FULFILLING

First published 1952
Second Edition (revised and enlarged) 1955
Third Edition (revised and enlarged) 1960

Frontispiece DOROTHY KERIN AND BABY ANNE, 194

FULFILLING

A SEQUEL TO

THE LIVING TOUCH

by

DOROTHY KERIN

with Foreword by
The Bishop of Coventry

ACKNOWLEDGEMENTS

The illustrations of Miss Kerin and Baby Anne and of Miss Kerin and her Adopted Children are from photographs by Lenare. Chapel House, Ealing is from a water-colour sketch by K. Laurence; Chapel House, Speldhurst from a photograph by E. Waterfield and Burrswood from a drawing by V. Roberts.

Printed in Great Britain by
The Courier Printing and Publishing Co., Ltd.
Tunbridge Wells, Kent

CONTENTS

LIST OF ILLUSTRATIONS

FOREWORD

By The Bishop of Coventry

What a welcome relief to pass from the shadowy to the real, to turn from the realm of the hypothetical to the world of experience. This is a book of personal experience, a book which describes the meeting of God with man. Here, in page after page of thrilling (but humble) personal experience, we come face to face with a living, loving God. The writer speaks of a God she knows. She does not offer pious platitudes or theoretical propositions. She offers facts of evidence. She witnesses to what she knows to be true.

She tells of a God who enters men's lives to heal, to make whole, to make holy. She writes of miracles, works of wonder. To a world that has lost hope she offers the hope of a living Christ. To a world that has lost its way, she points to a Light that shines, and shining guides. To meet God is to be consoled, but also to be challenged.

This is the story of a ministry of consolation, wrought by God through one who is prepared to trust Him to the hilt. But this trusting is a challenge to us ordinary mortals who love to have our haversacks filled with rations before we set forth upon our journey.

FOREWORD

The Bible is the story of a God who speaks to men on the journey, as they journey. We must start that journey in faith, believing that guidance from God will be given as we go.

Such was the discovery of the widow of Serepta. As she obeyed and set forth upon the journey of obedience, she discovered that there was always enough meal at the bottom of the barrel, ever enough oil at the bottom of the cruse.

Such has been the discovery of Miss Kerin. She has gone forward in faith and her Lord has provided—not always without trial and testing—but always to complete fulfilment.

Those who have had the privilege of meeting Miss Kerin, who have visited her beautiful house, who have met her family of nine children, we know how fully the writer of this book has lived out a detached life of devoted service. She gives herself without stint to a needy world. Long may she be spared to continue her ministry among us.

I am proud to be associated with the late Bishop of St. Alban's in paying my tribute to a very wonderful woman at work in the ministry of healing.

CUTHBERT BARDSLEY

I

How it all Began

To those who are acquainted with my book entitled *The Living Touch*, which was published by G. Bell in 1914, in which an account of the miraculous healing vouchsafed to me by God is recorded, there will be little need of explaining the reason of writing this book " FULFILLING ", which is written with a sense of deep gratitude and humility to the Glory of God.

Many have long felt that the time has come to place on record some of the wonderful events and healings of body, mind and spirit, which have taken place since the publishing of *The Living Touch*, and that the time is NOW.

It is my earnest prayer and hope that what is written in the following pages will not merely interest the reader into whose hands the book may perchance fall, but that it may be blessed and used of God to reawaken a faith in God's plan for the healing of those who are sick in body or mind.

For those who are not acquainted with *The Living Touch*, these extracts from the Introduction may be of interest, or by way of establishing a framework for the present book.

Much has been written of my miraculous Healing which took place on 18th February 1912. I fear that, in almost every instance, inaccuracy and exaggeration have crept in, for which I am in no way responsible.

After many years of hopeless invalidism I was completely and instantaneously healed by Our Beloved Lord Jesus Christ. This experience, I feel, was not meant for me alone, but for the strengthening of man's Faith in Divine Healing. With my restoration to health God has given me, as you will see as you read what follows, the work of proclaiming the fact that He still, as when on Earth, cares for the health and well-being, not only of the soul, but of the body. Through Faith and Prayer we shall receive these great blessings.

I am frequently questioned as to whether I attribute my recovery to any of the recognized systems of Healing? With the exception of my regular physicians, who in turn had pronounced my case hopeless, no one was attempting to cure me. Healing by hypnotism, the help of friendly spirits, Christian Science, suggestive therapeutics, etc., had no part in bringing about my restoration to Health. My Healing came direct from God, and God alone; to HIM be the Glory. There was no earthly intermediary.

God is the same yesterday, to-day and forever.

The miracles Our Lord performed in Galilee, and along the Jordan two thousand years ago, He can, and still does, to-day. There was not one God for the first century and another for the twentieth. Miracles of Healing and the re-creation of new life are happening to-day, but many of us shut our eyes to them.

The New Testament is full of promises of Healing and I am confident that as soon as we open our spiritual eyes, in Faith, we shall see their fulfilment. We have built up barriers between spiritual realities and ourselves by unbelief and worldliness. But as soon as we allow these barriers to be broken down by the Love of God, and ourselves to be made receptive, there will be a great inrush of the Holy Spirit, and we shall receive His bountiful gifts, which are the true inheritance of all Christians, purchased for us by our Saviour Jesus Christ.

All unworthy as I am, I have been permitted to see and realize the great Love of Jesus. What He has graciously done for me should be a living testimony of His Love. Whereas I was once prostrate, now I am well, every whit whole, a humble instrument in His hands, to manifest and bear witness to God. The Health and Happiness that have come to me are so complete, that the pain and suffering of past years are obliterated from my memory.

There is nothing of importance or interest to relate during my childhood, which was spent with my parents and brothers and sister. Up to the age of twelve years my life was full of happiness. Especially have I to thank God for giving me spiritual joy and a feeling of His Presence ever with me, which I had, ever since I can remember anything.

In 1902 my father died, and from this time it was observed that my health was quickly failing. The Doctor was consulted, in whose care I was eventually for four years, spending most of my time in bed, or lying out of doors.

In 1907 I caught a chill which terminated in pneumonia. My life was despaired of and for two weeks I hovered between life and death. Many prayers were offered on my behalf which were answered. My partial recovery came about immediately after receiving the Blessed Sacrament. I was unable to leave my bed after this illness, and was examined by other doctors who, after bacteriological examinations, diagnosed my illness as phthisis. From this time onwards, until my healing, namely, five years later, I was almost completely bedridden.

During this period I was taken to various hospitals, nursing homes, sanatoriums, where the doctors were of opinion that, unless there was immediate change for the better, I should not live more than a few months. Severe haemorrhages were constant, and many were the times when the end was expected. I was nursed almost entirely by my mother, with the help of a visiting nurse.

The last of twenty-eight doctors had said there was no hope of recovery; everything humanly possible had been done, and my friends were just waiting for Jesus to call me.

On December 26th tubercular peritonitis set in, and for the next four weeks I was often unconscious and, according to the doctors, blind, this being due, they said, to tubercular meningitis.

On February 17th Dr. Norman warned my mother that death might come at any moment, and that he thought it unlikely that I should live through the night. Of all this, however, I was oblivious, for Our Beloved Lord in His Love did not let me know the terrors of blindness, but showed me spiritual realities. This time was to me one beautiful day, passed in an indescribably lovely place, where everything, both to see and to feel, was exquisite harmony. It was at the end of this, my beautiful day, that Jesus made manifest His healing power in my body, and raised me up from my bed of sickness every whit whole, strong in every organ and limb.

MY BEAUTIFUL DAY

On Sunday morning, February 4th, I received the Blessed Sacrament, and as the priest came towards my bed with the chalice, I saw a golden light radiating from it which enveloped the priest. I had never seen this before, though all through my illness I had made my communion once a month, sometimes more often. It was a beautiful experience. The Divine Presence was indeed a reality. When the service was over, everything around me seemed to grow dim and misty and I could not see anything clearly. In the evening I asked my little sister to sing " Abide with me ": it was all so dark. She did not know it well enough to sing, but, as she sat by my bed, her hand in mine, we heard it sung from beginning to end so beautifully. My sister heard it as distinctly as I did, and said: " Oh how wonderful!" We were certain it must have been the Holy Angels singing, for there was no one singing in the house or outside. After this I seemed to drift into space, no longer conscious of my body but my spirit overflowing with joy and love, and a transcendent feeling of supreme happiness impossible to describe in human language. I passed on and on. As I went the way grew brighter and brighter until I saw in front of me a wonderful Altar, formed, as it were, by Angels. There were six at the back and one in front, more beautiful than the rest. He was holding a chalice from which he gave me to drink. They all disappeared; as they went they chanted words which I could not understand. I passed on again, and soon I heard a great flocking sound, and saw, coming from every direction, white-robed figures. Some of them were carrying lilies, some had haloes. Their movements made lovely music; they all looked as though they were coming and going with some definite purpose. No words of mine can express or exaggerate the exquisite beauty of the scene. As I looked I saw One coming towards me. I thought He was coming for me and held out my hands towards Him, but He smiled and said, " No, Dorothy, you are not coming yet." Again I passed on; this time I seemed to go a much greater distance, until I could go no further, when I heard a voice say " Dorothy " three times. I answered, " Yes, I am listening. Who is it?" Then a great light came all around me and an Angel took my hand in His and said, " Dorothy, your sufferings are over. Get up and walk." He passed His hands over my eyes and touched my ears, and then I opened my eyes and found myself sitting up in bed. My mother and a number of friends were standing around my bed, all looking very frightened, and some clutching at each other. It all seemed so strange to me and I could not understand why they were all there. I asked for my dressing-gown, telling them that I was quite well, and that I must get up and walk. They were all too astonished to speak or move.

The Angel again said to me, " Get up and walk." They brought the dressing-gown. When I had put it on I got out of bed unassisted. Part of the light which emanated from the Angel came to the right side of my bed. I put my hand on it, and it led me out of the room, along a passage and back into my bedroom. Though I had not walked for nearly five years, I now walked quite steadily, not the least bit shaky; indeed I felt well and strong and might never have been ill at all. Soon I realized I was hungry and asked for food. They brought me milk in a feeding cup, which I refused, finally going in search of food myself down two flights of stairs, returning with a real meal. How I enjoyed it, too! It was the first solid food I had been able to digest for a long time and I had not the slightest pain or discomfort after eating it. There were sixteen people in my room all very mystified and amazed at what they saw. I was perfectly well. ALL pain had left me, my sight was restored, and I felt better and stronger than I can ever remember feeling before. It was half-past nine in the evening when I got up, and at twelve o'clock, midnight, I went back to bed, and slept until eight o'clock the following morning. When I got up, my mother and friends, who knew that I had been like a skeleton the day before, were amazed to see my body quite normal and in a perfect condition. I was quite plump, all my bones being covered with firm, healthy flesh. This in the space of twelve hours! Blessed be God.

At nine o'clock Dr. Norman was sent for. When he heard that I was up and well, he thought it must be a mistake, and came to the house post-haste, expecting to find that I had passed away. On entering my room, he asked my mother what it all meant? I ran to meet him, and he turned to my mother and said, "Is it possible that this is the girl I left dying yesterday?" As soon as he had recovered from the shock he examined me and pronounced me perfectly healthy and well. He then asked me to go up a steep flight of stairs to test the strength of my muscles. When he saw me run up, he said, " Great God, what is the meaning of it all?"

When approached as to the cause of my present condition, he could give no explanation, but said it was certainly the most marvellous recovery he had known during the course of his experience. Next day he made the following statement, published in the *Daily Chronicle* of February 22nd:

" When I heard the girl had got up and was about the house I would not believe it until I had been to see for I left her on Saturday night apparently dying." Asked " Did she really suffer from consumption and diabetes?" he replied, " Oh certainly, there is no question whatever about that." " Then what is your theory?" asked the representative, " as to the cause of her present condition?"

" I have no theory," he replied. " Had I read of it, I certainly should not have believed it. She is well, but how she got better I don't know."

In an interview with an *Evening News* representative, Dr. Norman stated that " he had always hoped that the girl might recover, but that on Saturday he gave up hope. She had suffered enough to kill half-a-dozen people," he said. " In attending her he had found all the gravest symptoms of advanced tuberculosis, of diabetes, and other complications. She had been attended, under him, by twelve nurses up to the present, and a chart was kept of her temperature. This chart shows that her temperature rose and fell in the most alarming way . . . sometimes reaching as high as 105."

This statement was published in *The Evening News*, 20th February 1912.

At the request of Dr. Norman, a number of medical men examined me and were amazed when they heard the past history of my case, and admitted that my healing was something beyond their ken. A fortnight later I was examined by two X-ray specialists, and found by them to be perfectly well.

Tests for the presence of tubercle both by Von Pirquet's and Calmetté's methods made by Dr. Murray Leslie were negative, no reaction being produced in either case.

Three days after my healing, I was invited by Dr. Edwin Ash to his home in Seymour Street, that I might receive rest and quiet, away from the crowds of people who constantly came to see me, many from mere curiosity. I remained with Dr. Ash for several weeks. It was here that God revealed the purpose of my healing to me. I had prayed much that God would guide me into the way of His Will, and show me what He had brought me back to do, and was waiting in Faith for His guidance, when it was made quite clear in a vision.

On Sunday, March 11th, I was roused from sleep by a voice saying " Dorothy". I sat up, and saw at the foot of my bed, a wonderful light, out of which came the most beautiful face of a woman. She was holding a lily in her hand, and came quite close to my side saying, " Dorothy, you are quite well now. God has brought you back to use you for a great and privileged work. In your prayers and faith, many sick shall you heal; comfort the sorrowing; give faith to the faithless. Many rebuffs will you have, but remember you are thrice blessed. His Grace is sufficient for you. He will never leave you."

After making the sign of the Cross over me with her lily she disappeared. When I awoke in the morning, the scent of her lily still remained.

The answer to my prayer had come. All unworthy as I am, God has a work for me to do. I pray that He will empty of self, and make more worthy, the very imperfect channel He has chosen.

After this vision there came a period of waiting, when one had to possess one's soul in patience. It was not easy to be still and wait when there were so many in spiritual darkness and sickness waiting for the light of God's Love to illuminate their hearts and minds, and heal their bodies. The longing to share the joy of my new-found health grew day by day, and in His own way and time God made this possible. The way of ministration was being made clear, and one learnt that the Gifts of God can only be received through prayer and faith in accordance with His Will. True spiritual joy comes to us through communion with God, and bodily health and peace of mind follow, as growth follows rain and sunshine. In Him is no darkness. If we put our hands in His, and by His grace, follow in His footsteps, we shall know the truth and realize the wonderful power of the Love that is infinite. We can live in the very presence of God, in the midst of the promised land. We are no longer pilgrims and strangers, but can, here and now, enter into our inheritance as heirs of the Kingdom of God.

A TESTIMONY TO "THE LIVING TOUCH"

BY GEORGE F. C. SEARLE, SC.D., F.R.S.

Formerly University Lecturer in Experimental Physics, Cambridge, sometime Fellow of Peterhouse; Bishop's (lay) Reader, Diocese of Ely

I BEGAN to teach Experimental Physics at the Cavendish Laboratory, Cambridge, in 1888. About 1907, nervous trouble began to disturb me. This increased and, at times, I was unable, for a few days, to do my work. In October 1910, I was ordered from Cambridge at one-and-a-half hour's notice. My wife and I went to London to relatives, and there Sir Henry Head, F.R.S., ordered me to go to a nursing home in Ventnor. After that we were to go to Jamaica. I was seven weeks in the home. In Januray 1911, we sailed for Jamaica. After some weeks we went on to Bermuda, New York and Nova Scotia. We got back to the Isle of Wight in July. We returned to Cambridge in October 1911, for me, as we hoped, to resume my work as Demonstrator and Lecturer in Physics. But the old trouble returned and, for a fortnight, I was worse than at any previous time. The symptoms gradually passed off, and I was able to begin work again, but for the next three years I was liable to disabling spells of nervous weakness. Normally, my work was heavy as I had to deal with large classes of students.

In November 1914 I found Dorothy's book, *The Living Touch*, in a shop in Cambridge. I had, from childhood, believed in miracles but the book brought me up against them in a new and intense way. I read it many times and, as a very happy result, the old weakness left me, and I have been a " young " man since that time. I was pensioned off, under an age limit, in 1935, but on account of the war I went back to work in January 1940 and continued until October 1945, when the return of other teachers from war work set me free.

I was eighty-seven on 3rd December 1951. I am thankful to say that I am lively and in good health. I am grateful for this opportunity of expressing my thanks to God for the help sent me through *The Living Touch*.

My wife and I have had Dorothy's friendship since 1915 and we have been many times to Chapel House, Ealing. She stayed with us in 1915 and 1916. I am thankful for that friendship and for all that Dorothy has taught me. But all this was later than 1914. It was *The Living Touch* which was the dynamite.

I have made the book known to many people.

Some have been aided directly by the book itself. Others have gone further and have received help through friendship with Dorothy and through her ministry to those needing succour for soul or body.

In the last few years, public thought about Healing has greatly changed. For a long time, it was commonly held to be all nonsense. But now, " healing " is " in the air ", and people are ready to think it will be easy for them to be healed. There is a danger that this search for healing may encourage persons to set up as " healers " without recognizing the need of a change of heart and the forsaking of sin.

Dorothy's attitude is clear. She does not make light of sin and would declare that people must repent of their sins, if they are serious in seeking Healing. She proclaims the Lord Jesus Christ as the Lover and Redeemer of sinners, and, as I see it, her life is used in leading people to love Him and to rest in His love. But, as Jesus declared many times that all the " works " He did were really the works of His Father, so she realizes that all Healings are the work of God, the Father Almighty. His Being and His will must have the chief place in the lives of those who seek Healing. This may require the acceptance of an illness, but, when acceptance ousts discontent, a frequent and a very potent cause of the continuance of illness is removed.

In 1952 I stayed at " Burrswood " for three days as Dorothy's guest. From the Visitors' Book and in other ways I realized anew something of the range of her appeal. Of many nationalities and of many faiths, people have come from many countries at all times of day and night, seeking help for their bodies, or, more importantly, for their souls.

Dorothy's own life is set in the Church of England. She has adopted the Collect for the Sixth Sunday after Trinity as the " Chapel House Prayer ". It has been used since A.D. 500, but it gives a living picture of " Chapel House " and " Burrswood ", and may well serve as a guide to those who read this book.

The constant influx of people desiring interviews and ministrations makes very heavy demands on Dorothy. If no account were taken of the Divine help which can come to those who serve God without reserve, it would be wonderful how she has kept alive. Time has shown that as her need is, so is her strength. Nearly twenty years ago, several attacks of influenza left her very weak. When I saw her, she let out a great secret by saying " What a lovely thing it is to feel that you have come to the end of all your own strength!"

For years Dorothy has had enough to do. A surprise came when, about 1940, she legally adopted nine children, four boys and five girls, who needed a parent's love and care. They are now at school. Perhaps only those who know how God can provide for those who trust Him, will not wonder how the money for the school fees—and for other purposes—is found.

A TESTIMONY

These words are written to make known, not Dorothy's obvious needs, but the goodness of God, the All-knowing, in supplying them. A few words may help some readers here. In 1915, a Research Student, now a Professor, came to me to discuss his future. He was anxious and troubled. He saw Dorothy for a few minutes. I told him that, if he were trustful, an answer would come in two or three days. Next morning, I had only one letter. It asked me to recommend a man of just his type. The letter had been posted *before* he came to me. " *Before* they call, I will answer " (Isaiah 65, 24). Years ago a woman had bad noises in the head. Hands were laid on her with prayer. Several days later she asked the Lord to heal her. Next morning she awoke healed. When I saw her later, she said with glee, " It is only those who trust the Lord who know how good He is!" I had the happiness of being at the dedication of Chapel House, by Dr. Hough, Bishop of Woolwich, on 25th October 1930 as well as at the dedication of " Burrswood " by Bishop Loyd of St. Alban's on 15th September 1948.

May God bless this book to His glory and to the help of many.

Cambridge
25th July 1952

II

St. Raphael's

In 1915 I was invited by Dr. and Mrs. Langford-James to go and make my home with them, where the necessary quiet and peace could be provided for me, to wait upon God, for the unfolding of His plan. I accepted this, I believed, God-sent offer; and lived with them, as their adopted daughter, for the following fourteen years. During these years much happened in preparation for the work God has given me to carry out since, and in my humble endeavour to give to the world a record of this work, I have only one desire, that is, that it may be used to God's Glory.

I pray that those who read this little book, may lose sight of Dorothy Kerin, who is nothing, who has nothing, who can do nothing, except offer herself to God, as a bit of pipe, through which He can pour Himself.

During the years 1915–29, I lived in simple vows, under the direction of Dr. Langford-James. I owe much to his wise guidance, and to his care for the development of my spiritual life. For this I am profoundly grateful, and for all the help he gave me, and above all, for the long spells of quiet and prayer he made possible for me to delight in.

As time passed God's plan unfolded and, as it were, a framework was built up, upon which a Home of Healing was established. The increasing number of those who came seeking healing, both of body and mind, made it abundantly clear that some centre would have to be found, where these seekers and sufferers could come. It had always been the dream and hope of Dr. Langford-James, and many others, that, one day, God would give me such a centre.

In 1929, the dawn of this hope came, when I knew that God was calling me to a more active life in the world. The possibility of renting a small house was presented to me and, after waiting upon God in prayer for His guidance, it seemed to me made clear that I was to make this venture of faith, which I did.

The difficulties and frustrations which followed this decision were many, and at times seemed almost insurmountable, when continuing to have Faith was indeed hard work. But, one by one, these difficulties were overcome, and eventually St. Raphael's, as it was called, came into being. (It was a modest house, containing ten rooms, in Culmington Road, Ealing.) It was dedicated to God as a thanksgiving for my Healing, by Bishop

Boutflower. How was it to be achieved? Where was the money to come from for repairs, alterations, furnishings, etc.? I did not know. Of one thing only was I certain, that God had shown me that He wanted it.

In a wonderful way gifts arrived: offers of help from many directions, gifts and loans of furniture, until, to the amazement of all, it was complete. It was very sweet and simple. People told me they felt the spirit of love and beauty radiating from this little centre, which had become so full of the peace of God. The tiny Chapel at the top of the house was the power point, and how well I remember the first time the Bishop of Nasik (Bishop Loyd) came to celebrate the Holy Mysteries there. It was an exquisitely beautiful service. There were only five people present, and indeed, it would not have been possible to hold any more. The Bishop turning towards us, his face shining with the glory of God, said in his little address: "It is Thy Father's good pleasure to give unto Thee the Kingdom. . . ." What a prophecy this truly was, and how often, during the years that followed, have I been reminded of this promise; for promise it surely was.

Since the blessing of St. Raphael's the house has been full to overflowing with those who have come seeking healing, of body and mind. Many have felt the healing touch of Our Blessed Lord upon them, and many have found, and gone away with His Peace in their hearts. God is using this little centre more and more, and it has become too small to hold all those who want to come. What could we do to enlarge its borders? God had the plan all ready made, and in a short space of time it came into being.

It was during a walk with Bruno, my red setter, that I felt curiously drawn to a house that we passed day by day, on our way to Walpole Park, where Bruno delighted in his daily exercises. I had no idea that this old derelict house could concern me in any way, and had I realized, all at once, that Our Divine Lord had a so much bigger task for me to attempt, I might have feared my ability to achieve this. But He has made it abundantly clear that this is His Will, and it was born in upon me that I must go and see, and investigate Chapel House. This I did. At once came the conviction that it was God's House, planned and prepared by Him, for some work He meant to do there. I did not know what part, if any, He might have for me to do in it. But it came quite unmistakably, that Our Lord meant it for an enlarged St. Raphael's. As I left the grounds I heard clearly " The Lord is King ". These words rang in my ears the whole way home. I went into the little Chapel and prayed that God would show me what was His will in the matter. " Get it for Me." This was the answer that came. I knew that voice, and I knew that, come what may, I should, by the grace of God, obey it and fulfil His command, " Get it for Me."

Of course the whole thing seemed, on the face of it, the wildest of impossibilities, for the bare purchase price was between four and five thousand. There was very little in the bank, and little St. Raphael was only just making two ends meet, and was being kept going by various gifts and thank-offerings, leaving no margin for a larger venture, however great the need.

The absolute certainty about Chapel House remained with me, in spite of all my common-sense reasonings, and those of my friends. I asked Our Lord to give me a sign if He wished me to embark on this venture. I prayed that He would make it possible for me to pay off the debt that still remained on St. Raphael's. I waited with the growing conviction that God would give this sign. It came on the third day. A friend wrote:

" My dear, I have received some unexpected dividends, and feel God asks me to send it to you. I have no doubt you will find some good use for it."

Here was the sign. Thanks be to God! I asked the Bishop of Nasik, who was then in England, to come and see the house, for I trusted his wise and God-given advice and counsel so utterly, and knew that he would help me to see, and do, God's will. The Bishop came and told me afterwards that he had come " prepared to bring his common sense to bear upon me and save me from committing myself to so rash a venture ". Instead he felt, he said, that " the house was marked out in some special way, for Our Lord's service, and that he dare not incur the responsibility of disregarding this wonderful opportunity ".

The house takes its name from the Chapel once made and used there by the Walpole family, and to both of us it seemed as though Our Divine Lord Himself were speaking through the silence of the empty house, claiming to be owned and obeyed there as its Master. As we went from room to room they seemed to be not so much empty, as waiting; filled then and there with the summer sunshine, and waiting to be filled also with all the people and things that should bring back life to them. " Life that is Life indeed "... in other words " The Glory of the Lord."

As the Bishop and I knelt to say the " Gloria in excelsis " in the east room, which has one wall of the old Chapel, I think we were admitted into the fellowship of Angels, that have so signally guided and guarded all that has been undertaken since. We were both so conscious of unseen, but living active Presences. Perhaps they were some who had worshipped there, in the old Chapel, and who had made it their special prayer, that the Glory of the Lord should always fill that place, and shine forth from it. I believe the influence of their prayers has remained and lived on ever since.

All through July and August the problem of how the house was to be bought had to be faced, and at times it seemed a very difficult problem indeed, and when my courage was nearly failing some fresh mark of the Lord's goodness came to witness afresh to His unbounded Power to give. There were many praying that God would show me His plan, and on July 29th I made a definite offer to buy Chapel House. The owner, who was interested in the object for which I needed the house, had consented to accept £3,700, a very small sum for this most desirable freehold property. Then, of course, there would be a large sum needed to pay for the necessary repairs, alterations, furnishings, etc. Where was it all to come from? This was the question in many hearts and minds.

There was exactly nothing in hand towards this, save the certain knowledge that God wanted this house.

It was during these days of waiting upon God that we proved, "Where God guides, God provides."

We were now in the week of the sixth Sunday after Trinity, and in the Collect for this week we find the perfect prayer to use for Chapel House, and all those who shall come to give help and receive it.

"O God, Who hast prepared for them that love Thee such good things as pass man's understanding: Pour into our hearts such Love toward Thee, that we, loving Thee above all things, may obtain Thy promises, which exceed all that we can desire; Through Jesus Christ Our Lord."

Gifts started to arrive; promises of help of every sort and kind; offers of furniture, pictures, etc.; one gift which remains on the Altar to this day came from a poor woman who said, " I am so thankful to God for all He has done for me, I want to give you my most precious possession, and I pray that He will bless and multiply it a thousandfold.". . . This gift was a Jubilee florin, which had been given to this woman by her mother at her confirmation. It was surely precious in God's sight. For He did multiply it a thousandfold and more. Then came a loan of £200, which was offered to God in faith, and represented the entire capital of a Missionary, who felt that God had asked her to lend it to Him. Gifts of this sort continued to pour in, until all the necessary money had been collected, with the exception of £500. This my bank promised to advance, on my undertaking to repay this by mid-December. I was so sure of God's guidance that I was able to give this undertaking fearlessly.

By the middle of October the house was ready for occupation. Miracles had certainly been achieved in a short time, and gloom and dirt had given way to beauty and harmony.

The way of the Lord had been made ready for Him to pour upon Chapel House the fullness of His Blessing.

The Bishop of Woolwich, who had taken a great interest in all these happenings, and to whose prayers I am sure we owe so much, had promised to come and dedicate the house on October 25th.

Every preparation had been made with this aim in view, and on the eventful day, the house appeared as a bride, all glorious in her apparel.

Many were conscious of the presence of the Holy Angels and of countless, though unseen, hosts, all helping together, with joy, to prepare the way of the Lord. The house was a bower of flowers, and cheery fires glowed from every hearth, in warm welcome of the large gathering which assembled to take part in the offering of Chapel House to God, for Him to use as He willed, for the healing and refreshment of all who should come seeking His good gifts.

The Bishop, robed in Cope and Mitre, gave a short address, expressing his hope (and indeed that of many) that here, in Chapel House, God would find Faith and Hope: the Faith that would enable Him to give abundantly of His good gifts; and that in all we were doing this day in His name, we must remember, that the light of the knowledge of the Glory of God, was shining full upon us in the face of Jesus Christ, our ever-present Lord and King. " Thou art the King of Glory, O Christ " is the thought which calls us each one here to-day to a very definite seeking of His Sovereignty. There are possibilities beyond all that we can desire, and all that we know how to ask, which the King of Love will bring to pass, if our wills are set steadily upon seeking first the supremacy of His sovereign will, in all things when we pray.

To face page 34

CHAPEL HOUSE, EALING

At the end of the address, the Bishop went into the Chapel with his Chaplain and asked the assembled congregation to join in singing the Veni Creator, as a prayer:

Come, Holy Ghost, our souls inspire,
And lighten with celestial fire;
Thou the anointing Spirit art,
Who dost Thy sevenfold gifts impart;

Thy blessed unction from above
Is comfort, life, and fire of love;
Enable with perpetual light
The dullness of our blinded sight:

Anoint and cheer our soiled face
With the abundance of Thy grace:
Keep far our foes, give peace at home;
Where Thou art Guide no ill can come.

Teach us to know the Father, Son,
And Thee, of Both, to be but One;
That through the ages all along
This may be our endless song,

Praise to Thy eternal merit,
Father, Son, and Holy Spirit. Amen.

He then prayed: "Almighty and merciful God, Who has granted such Grace unto Thy Bishops and Priests, that whatsoever they do fitly, in Thy name, is held to be done by Thee. We entreat Thy great goodness, that Thou wouldest visit whatsoever we shall visit, and bless whatsoever we shall bless, and grant that, as we enter this place, in lowliness of heart, all evil may be put to flight, and the Angels of Peace enter in, through Jesus Christ Our Lord. Amen.

" O Lord protect this House and let Thy Holy Angels guard it and drive away all evil from it."

We then said together the 121st Psalm:

I will lift up mine eyes unto the hills: from whence cometh my help.
My help cometh even from the Lord: who hath made heaven and earth.
will not suffer they foot to be moved: and He that keepeth thee will not sleep.
Behold, he that keepeth Israel; shall neither slumber nor sleep.
The Lord himself is thy keeper. The Lord is thy defence upon thy right hand:
So that the sun shall not burn thee by day: neither the moon by night.
The Lord shall preserve thee from all evil: yea, it is even he that shall keep thy soul.
The Lord shall preserve thy going out, and thy coming in: from this time forth for evermore.

After which the Bishop proceeded to visit every room, praying a special prayer in each. On reaching the dining-room, he prayed:

" O God the Father of all the families of the earth, we humbly beseech Thee on behalf of this house, which we now dedicate to Thee for all who shall dwell therein, and for all things within it. That it may please Thee to bless and hallow this place and fill it with Thy goodness. Grant O Lord, to those who shall dwell therein, all things necessary and requisite, as well for the body as for the soul. Therefore at our going in, bless and hallow this house, even as Thou wast pleased to bless the House of David. Let the Angels of Light dwell within its walls and guard the inhabitants of this dwelling. Through Jesus Christ our Lord. . . ."

The Bishop blessed each bedroom, and prayed:

" Save us, O Lord, waking and guard us sleeping, that awake we may be with Christ, and in Peace we may take our rest."

As many as could followed the Bishop back to the Chapel where, after singing the general thanksgiving, the Bishop gave his blessing. He then called me to him and laid his hands upon my head, asking God to bless me specially for this work He had called me to do.

It was a wonderful moment in which I felt our Lord had taken the Bishop's hands in His own hands, to bless me.

After the blessing of the House we all assembled in the dining-room for tea, when the Bishop asked me to go quietly with him to the Chapel, as he had something to tell me. We went and both knelt down; the Bishop prayed that God would guide, guard, and strengthen us, not only for the immediate work of Chapel House but for all that was to grow out of this work in the future. When he had finished praying, the Bishop told me that he saw the house next to Chapel House joined on, and was sure, in God's own time, this would come to pass. At that moment it seemed like an inner voice, saying " Not only one . . . but ALL." . . . I saw the whole side of Mattock Lane, which contained five other houses, the large gap between the first house on the left, filled up with a building, and I knew that God had, then and there, set His seal upon them. And in the fullness of time this vision was fulfilled, as you will read as this story continues.

The early days of Chapel House were fraught with many difficulties of every kind. Continuing to have faith was hard work, and those were the days when one went on not daring to do anything, except just trust God and leave it all to Him. They were days when He said so often: " Is My Hand shortened at all, that it cannot redeem?" What blessed words of hope and comfort, and what certainty of His care of, and love for, us. In those days of testing we learned to trust Him, and the Faith which He had given us grew into knowledge.

There were many wonderful healings of body, mind and spirit, and God was pouring upon the work of Chapel House His boundless gifts and blessings. The financial position was, at times, acute, but all that was necessary came, often at the eleventh hour. But the cruse of oil never ran day.

We were gettting towards the end of November, when Bishop Loyd wrote from India asking how the money was coming in for the repayment to the Bank. I had to answer that at the time of writing I had exactly £80, this being the Thank-offering of one who was healed. Beyond this I did not know of any further help, only I was sure that if Chapel House was God's will (as I most devoutly believed it to be) then He would provide. And upon this belief I waited in Faith.

On December 3rd Bruno became desperately ill. In the Vet.'s opinion he was dying from some poison he had picked up. All through that day and night I nursed and tended him, with very little apparent result. He became weaker and weaker. The following day he was just alive and by night I had to carry him upstairs. I must confess to a very sad and sorrowful heart, for Bruno had been my constant companion and friend, and we loved each other well and truly. He was almost human with a most amazing understanding. He had come to be known as "The Brown Verger" and attended ALL the services in Chapel. Everybody loved him, and the thought of his not being with us any more was one that had to be faced with courage.

I was sitting on the floor, with his head pillowed on my lap, thinking and praying about the problem of finding the money for the bank. Suddenly I was aware of Our Lord's Divine Presence and heard the voice I knew so well, saying, " Fear not, I will provide all thy need." I was then aware of Bruno, who was in an ecstasy of delight, standing up wagging his tail, QUITE restored. I told him we must go down to Chapel to thank God for his healing, which we did.

As I prayed in thanksgiving from a full heart, I became aware that God had promised to provide all the need. I knew this was a test of my faith. I went to my study and wrote the cheque for £500 for the bank, dating it December 13th, and placed this upon the altar. The song of joy and thanksgiving was in my heart. Not that I had doubted God's power to send the money but because it was to me His seal of approval. I returned to bed and slept. In the morning the joy was still singing in my heart, and I expect was visible on my face, for my mother asked: " What has happened to make you so happy?" I told her about Bruno, and then added, "AND the cheque is on the Altar!—ready for Our Lord to honour." Shall we blame her if in her anxiety, she felt that this was perhaps only Dorothy's wish? However, nothing could have shaken my belief, for I knew the Beloved had promised.

I received a letter from a friend who had been touched and healed by our Lord, in which she sent a cheque for £100, knowing that God had inspired her to do this. This offering implied a great act of faith and meant much to this woman, who was certainly not blessed with an abundance of this world's goods . . . but she had her reward.

The next day I received two more letters, one containing a cheque for £200, one £100, and both givers saying: " God has guided me to send you this—you will know why." This made £480.

On the morning of the 13th—the day due for the cheque to be paid—I received from an unknown source a cheque for £20, this enabling me to post the cheque which God had honoured for His work.

This is only one of many such happenings during the early years of Chapel House. God, in His goodness ALWAYS supplied the need.

There will not be time or space to record all these wonderful signs of God's presence, and power with us, but you will see, as you read, how this work, begun in faith for His Glory, has been abundantly justified.

There were those who took an unfair advantage of the fact that no fixed charge was made for care and residence in the Home. There had been such a succession of these careless receivers who had no idea of being givers also . . . and this was how the Home came to be registered as a Nursing Home.

Dr. Hopewell Ash, who was a specialist in Harley Street, came one day to see a patient he had in the Home, asking me if it were possible to take someone else. I replied, " I don't know how much longer the Home can go on if people do not give something towards the expenses." Whereupon he said: " Chapel House is far too valuable to us to allow anything to hinder the work being done here. I suggest you are registered as a Nursing Home and charge normal fees. This came as a shock to me, but after a time I did see that God's work could not be hindered by the fact that people were asked to do what they rightly should, and this would enable me to help many who could not otherwise come. So I applied for this licence, which was duly granted. A prospectus was drawn up stating that the Home was now a registered Nursing Home, where religion and medicine worked hand-in-hand. A list of names was given of those who sponsored the Home spiritually and medically. It may be of help and interest to some if I append the list.

His Grace The Archbishop of Canterbury.
His Grace The Archbishop of Corinth.

The Rt. Rev. The Bishop of Nasik.
The Rt. Rev. The Bishop Winnington-Ingram.
The Rt. Rev. The Bishop Boutflower.
Prebendary Wilson Carlile, C.H., D.D.
The Rev. R. Ll. Langford-James, D.D.
The Rev. H. S. Barrett, M.A.

REFERENCES

Dr. Hopewell-Ash, 8 Harley Street, W.1.

Dr. Leonard Browne, 9 Harley Street, W.1.

Lord Horder, 141 Harley Street, W.1.

Dr. Helena King, 102 The Avenue, W.5.

Maj.-Gen. Sir William Pike, K.C.B., Panton, Wragby, Lincs.

Dr. Burnett Rae, 93 Harley Street, W.1.

Dr. Maurice Wright, O.B.E., 86 Brook Street, W.1.

Vice-Admiral J. G. Armstrong, The United Services Club, S.W.1.

Sir George Arthur, M.V.O., The Carlton Club, S.W.1.

Lord Morven Cavendish Bentinck, Welbeck Abbey, Worksop, Notts.

Lady Boileau, Ketteringham Park, Wymondham, Norfolk.

Sir Roger Chance, MC., PH.D., The Athenaeum, S.W.1.

The Princess George Chavchavadze, 46 rue de Bellechasse, Paris, 7.

Maj.-Gen. H. A. Cummins, C.B., C.M.G., The United Services Club, S.W.7.

The Rt. Hon. Lord Daryngton, P.C., 65 Onslow Gardens, S.W.7.

The Dowager Lady Inchiquin, Dromoland Castle, Newmarket on Fergus, Ireland.

The Princess Achille Murat, 5 rue de Constantine, Paris, 7.

Dr. G. F. C. Searle, F.R.S., Wyncote, Hill's Road, Cambridge.

There is much that I feel should go into this book but I am being pressed to finish it. So I have decided to condense as much as possible and publish a fuller account of testimonies of healings in a later book.

The history of Chapel House abounds in causes for thankfulness, some of which I feel sure should be placed on record, and given to the world in the hope that the knowledge of these happenings may strengthen the faith of those who are seeking to know of God's living power, manifesting itself here with us to-day.

So many come to Chapel House and carry away new love for its Master and new trust in Him, as well as new thankfulness for the healing He has given. The dim eyes which have been blessed with renewed sight . . . deaf ears that have heard again . . . bed-ridden invalids who have gone away on their feet . . . troubled spirits and darkened minds that have found light and peace . . . " the Lord's doing " and " marvellous in our eyes ". Yet, even as we recall and give thanks for these mercies, there rises in our hearts the vision of still more wondrous gifts and benefits which He will give us when we are ready to receive them. There have been the material blessings also, and the privilege of being called upon to trust God in the dark. This trust has been more than justified . . . for all our needs have been supplied.

After the Home was registered as a Nursing Home, the work changed and we were asked to take many very sick patients who needed skilled nursing. A staff of nurses had to be engaged for this purpose, and among the many blessings vouchsafed to us, I count the coming of Miss Rose

Friend, as our Nursing Sister. She came in the first place seeking healing for herself, which in His own time and way, our Beloved Lord gave her. She then believed He had called her to come and serve Him in Chapel House, and answered this call and came. I have asked Miss Friend to write her own account of this, and also to give an account of some of the wonderful happenings she witnessed during the time she was Sister in Charge.

Then we have to thank God for sending to us our Hon. Chaplain, Father Barrett, Vicar of St. Barnabas, Ealing. It would take me many chapters to tell of all things he did for us, and for all those who came to stay at Chapel House. There are countless numbers of those who owe so much to him for great blessings received through his ministry and help. He was always unfailing in his love and giving, and personally I can never be grateful enough for God's good gift of him.

During the illness which helped me to trust in the unfailing goodness of God, he was never too tired to come after a long day's work, to pray with, and bless me. I know he will not wish me to enlarge upon his goodness and kindness, but there is much which I am sure has been written in the book of Life to his credit.

The time came when our Chapel was too small to hold all those who came, so it was decided to take the large room at the right-hand side of the front door and make that into a Chapel. This was done and it was blessed and dedicated by the Bishop of London, Dr. Winnington-Ingram. He permitted the Blessed Sacrament to be reserved permanently for the sick. This wonderful gift was of the kind which are " more than we can ask or think ". The Holy Mysteries were celebrated as often as possible in the Chapel, and those who were too ill to go to Chapel had the Blessed Sacrament brought to them in their rooms. So often patients have told me, " It was just as though the Lord Jesus came in at the door Himself." How true!

Father Barrett conducted a Meditation and Healing Service every Tuesday, and administered Holy Unction, and gave the laying on of hands to those who came seeking these administrations. There were many wonderful healings, some of which I shall record later on in this book. The days and weeks passed all too quickly. The volume of work was increasing and our accommodation was already inadequate, and the need for enlarging our boundaries was again an urgent one. This need had to be met and faced. How?

One night I had a vivid dream in which I saw the small Lodge at the gate turned into a little House where some of this need could be met. There was a fairly large garage built on to one side of the Lodge,

I found that this could be made into two rooms, thus giving us four more bedrooms, a sitting-room and bathroom. I discussed this possibility with the builders, who agreed that this could be done, and in a short space of time it was ready for use.

This helped us for a time, when again the need for yet more room was upon us. How could this be achieved? The need was there and one knew God had the plan . . . we must wait upon His guidance in prayer. This guidance came again in a dream, when I saw, not only the block of buildings I saw in the Chapel, on the day of the Blessing of Chapel House two years earlier, but the whole wing complete with interior decorations and furnishings. I prayed God to show me how this was to be made possible, and in a short time a cheque was sent to me to " use in any way I felt right for the enlarging of the possibilities of Chapel House ". This was surely God's way of showing me. I got plans made and passed by the local council and the work of building the new wing, which was called St. Faith's, was started.

St. Faith's was planned to give us six additional bedrooms, and two more bathrooms. The interior was carried out in light oak, with oak floors and large Crittal windows and central heating. The bedrooms were furnished in light oak with pastel shades of soft furnishings. People said it looked like a bit of Fairyland and it certainly was filled with light and peace.

On 18th February 1935, Lady Palmer came and laid the foundation stone, and on April 27th St. Faith's was blessed by Bishop Chandler and filled to capacity.

Very soon the need for further extension came, for the Home was always full and the demands of those writing to come increasing. Then came a time of testing. The big house on the right of Chapel House, " St. Michael's", the house Bishop Hough had seen as part of Chapel House, was in the market for sale. To many came the question: What did God mean us to do? How could it be made possible to see this vision fulfilled? Who could produce £6,000 to purchase it? I waited in prayer asking for God's guidance which came in two simple, but quite assuring words: " Not yet." . . . I knew that, come what may, in His own time God would fulfil this promise and St. Michael's WOULD be part of Chapel House.

To the dismay of many it was sold, and the new owner moved in, and to some that was the end of St. Michael's, as far as Chapel House was concerned. There remained, however, the promise I believed God had given, and this I kept in my heart.

The work continued to grow, and by now people were coming from many parts of the world, seeking to find the blessing of healing . . . if it should be God's will.

There were financial and other difficulties, and though God was pouring His blessings upon us, we were not left in any doubt as to the power of evil. We were beset with every kind of difficulty and frustration at times, and learnt that it was not easy or, alas! attractive, to do some of the hard things we were called upon to face and to do. But always one had the assurance that " My Grace is sufficient " and did this Grace ever fail or prove inadequate for the need? No never . . . thanks be to God.

III

Witness by Miss Rose Friend

I FIRST came to know of Dorothy Kerin at a tea party. I heard the story of her taking the old, derelict house and turning it into a beautiful House of Healing. The story had gripped me. An added impression was made a few days later when attending a " Quiet Day " I was told by three different people that if I didn't know Dorothy Kerin, I must.

The next free morning I telephoned and heard her voice. We made an appointment for that evening. That meeting closed a door in my life and opened one to perpetual joy, service and thanksgiving.

In 1930, Dorothy needed a Nursing Sister. We talked it over and agreed. I could not leave my home ties yet. . . . Nine months later I was seriously ill with high temperature, when it was decided for a surgeon to come and see me with a view to an operation. I asked for, and received the Laying on of Hands. . . . I knew our Lord was present. He touched me and I was healed.

I went to Chapel House to rest and get strong. What a lovely bit in my life that was! I didn't see much of Dorothy, but the whole house radiated Love and Peace, and when in the evenings she came, attended by her dog Bruno, it was verily the perfect ending to a perfect day.

My convalescence was short, and I returned to my home, constantly coming back to Chapel House at week-ends, and during one of these I was taken ill, and Dr. King diagnosed pneumonia. The third day I received the Laying on of Hands by the Chaplain and was instantly healed. . . . Dorothy was taken very ill with pleurisy, and I had been healed to nurse her.

It was a very wonderful privilege and experience to nurse Dorothy. She was a wonderful patient, always grateful, always thinking of others and, in spite of the utter weariness and extreme exhaustion, she endured, never a murmur . . . just endurance. But oh! the heartache for us! She got weaker and weaker . . . and one had to nurse her against such odds, as everyone round her—even the Chaplain—thought of, and spoke of, her as dying. Then a Specialist was called in for consultation and said: "As she was, she could not live for more than two months, but if she would have absolute rest for three months, she could pull through."

She was to be immovable. Think! Our quick-thinking, quick-moving Dorothy, to be immovable! . . . She made me pin her sleeve to the sheet to remind herself not to lift a hand!

Her recovery was slow but the whole time she never ceased to think of all the sufferers she had undertaken to pray for.

The house had emptied very much while she was ill, as folk naturally came for her help. So there was an added worry—lack of finance.

When all fever had left her, convalescence was sure and swift, and consequently the house filled.

Dorothy radiated Love, light and peace, and that means healing for so many.

There was one lady staying in the Nursing Home, who asked one day when Dorothy was out, " Miss Kerin is away to-day?"

I said, " How did you know? I wasn't telling anyone."

" Oh! I always know when she is in for I am conscious of a lovely golden light."

After Dorothy's convalescence, the way was open for me to accept her offer, and come as Nursing Sister. Oh! how gladly I responded to the call, and two sentences rang habitually in my ears: " Put off thy shoes from off thy feet for the ground on which thou standest is Holy " and " She must increase and I must decrease. . . ." That last was because my training had made me confident and assured, and I soon learnt that the love in Dorothy told her at once what each sufferer needed, far better than I with my set ideas, the result of a hospital training. I had to learn that Love ruled Chapel House. It was a wonderful lesson, and one that I am still learning.

There was a very hard and difficult road to walk when Dorothy continued her work after her severe illness. Her Faith and quiet assurance in God were wonderful, and bit by bit the obstacles vanished. And to cheer us on our way were the miracles of healing and wonder.

One of the many remarkable healings comes to mind. A Harley Street Specialist telephoned: " Would we take a case that had baffled several medical men? If Miss Kerin could take her it would be her last chance of recovery."

The patient came in an ambulance and was carried to bed prostrate. At the end of the first week she was distinctly better . . . a report was sent to the Specialist, who admitted that he was amazed at such a speedy betterment and said, " Continue what you are doing."

At the end of the second week the patient, who was sitting up in a chair, said: " I shall have to go home as I have no more money." " Don't worry, God will provide," was the answer: and the following morning she received a letter with another week's fees. She then began to walk and at the end of the third week was well. When her family arrived to take her home, they found her downstairs, radiant and walking. She went home and we heard later that she had at once taken on the housekeeping and cooking for them all.

One day I opened the front door to a weary looking little Indian lady, who said, " I have come to see Dorothy Kerin."

" I am sorry," I said. "She is away."

" Oh dear, and I have come all the way from India."

" Yes, but not only to see her."

Only to see her; I go back by the next boat."

It was arranged that she did see Dorothy before she left, and she went home, her fears having fallen from her, peace reigning in her heart, and praising God.

The little, nearly blind seamstress, who was working overtime by candlelight, had pricked her good eye and no longer could sew. She came straight up to London to see Dorothy Kerin. It was a very full day and I said, " I don't know that you can."

" I've come to see Dorothy Kerin, and here I sit till I do." When Dorothy heard she said, " Bring her in when there is a gap between two interviews, but you must come for her soon."

After a short time I went to the Chapel, and never will I forget that little ecstatic figure, hands clasped, face uplifted, chanting " I can see! I can see! Oh thank Him," and Dorothy kneeling behind her all light. . . . It was a wonderful miracle, and the little woman did what few remember to do—sent her thank-offering month after month, sixpence, and often a flower from her window-box.

Another came with great faith that God could heal her. She was in great pain always, and was to have an operation shortly. She received the Laying on of Hands but the pain was constant. Dorothy said quietly, " Have faith and wait." The sufferer thanked God for His blessing and waited. The day came for her visit to the surgeon to arrange about the operation; she left Chapel House in great pain. Dorothy said quietly, " Go in faith, God can heal you now." She went and, as she stood on the doorstep waiting to see the surgeon, the pain suddenly ceased. She was examined and the surgeon said, " There is no need to operate, your ear is healed."

There are innumerable instances which God has permitted me to witness, but there is only space here to give you a few of them. I cannot conclude, however, without telling of the remarkable experience of a reporter.

On the anniversary of Dorothy's miraculous healing it was quite usual for many reporters to arrive seeking copy for publication. On this occasion I had successfully got rid of seven, telling them of Miss Kerin's refusal to see them. Imagine my surprise and annoyance when, later in the day,

I found one of them sitting in the hall! I asked him what he was doing there? . . . to which he replied, " I promise you I have not come to get copy from Miss Kerin but help for my young brother, who is desperately ill in an asylum." He looked so earnest that I went to ask Miss Kerin if she could see him. To my surprise she said, " Yes, I will see him." He told her a tragic story of a young brother who was at that time certified and in a padded room. They went in to Chapel and there they both prayed. Miss Kerin took from her neck a small Crucifix, telling the man to take it to his brother. This man wrote shortly after, saying, " The next time I saw my brother I found him in a wild state, clearly possessed by an evil spirit. I held out the little cross to him, whereupon he became quiet, enabling me to talk reasonably to him." A week later the authorities wrote saying that he could be released because he was now quite well.

It is very wonderful working in a house that is verily God's, realizing so often that He is undertaking all things. The flowers, for instance! It was Easter Eve and funds were too low to buy lilies which were costly. Dorothy decided to use the flowers we had. It was the first Easter without lilies for the altar. Easter Eve, 7.30. . . . A knock on the front door and a large long box was brought in. Imagine our joy when we found lilies, abundant lilies, and a card from an American friend Dorothy had only seen once: " I was prompted to send you these lilies."

So many sense His presence and during the War years it was so often asked, " What is it in this house that is so different?". . . " I stand on the doorstep and feel all is peace and beauty." . . . " I feel all lifted up." . . . " I feel so different when I come here and I go away treading on air. . . ."

You will understand what a revelation it has been to me to work in Chapel House as a trained Nurse? I can and do testify to the fact that the blind have seen, the deaf have heard, the lame have walked, crooked limbs have been straightened, and the mentally deranged have found peace and sanity, and in many instances have resumed their normal work . . . and this often, after medical skill has pronounced them " incurable ".

ROSE FRIEND

IV

Difficulties and Triumphs

LIFE at this point had become very full when the days and nights seemed to hold only half the hours needed to answer all the demands made upon one. The house was full to capacity, some of the patients being very ill. There were many coming and going, everything appeared to be running in smooth gear, and for the moment at any rate, there was no ominous threatening of anything to disturb our peace.

I was tired and caught a chill, which eventually terminated in a sharp attack of pleurisy. Why God should have permitted this to happen at a time when I was so needed in the home was quite beyond my understanding. There was a reason, however, and in these weeks the mystery of pain and suffering was constantly in my mind. None of us can fully understand it, nor shall we whilst we are still on earth. It seemed to me that this sickness was not my own, but something to be shared and thrown into the common pool of suffering, and offered perhaps in some tiny way, as a drop in the filling up of the Cup.

One of the many blessings I have to thank God for, which came through this illness, was the coming of Dr. Helena King, who looked after me medically during this period. For the gift of her friendship and understanding and skill I could count this illness a very small price. Her unfailing care, and the giving of herself and her time . . . all this, and so much more which I know she will want to remain hidden, were blessings sent by God. But can any fail to appreciate why she became known as the beloved physician of Chapel House? Such she was, and in the years that followed her help and giving were unending, and never failed. I am not the only one who thanks God upon every remembrance of her.

My illness dragged on in spite of all that was done both spiritually and medically, and the time came when Dr. King felt she would like another opinion; whereupon Dr. Burrell was called in. He was then consultant to Brompton Hospital. His prognosis was, from my point of view, grave, for he ordered three months' rest, beginning with one month of " complete rest ".

By this, he explained to me, he meant, " Not even lifting a hand to feed myself ". I had given my promise to God, that I would accept whatever He would ask of me, and by His grace try to do. The days that followed were not easy, there were the times when one's spirit rebelled at this enforced inaction, there was so much waiting to be done. Then came the questioning in one's heart, " Oh God why must this be?" But often in these days I was reminded of His promise, " I will never leave thee."

Difficulties of every sort were piling up, and not the least of these, the debts which were accumulating. The Home was practically empty, for many said they would wait until I was well and then come. My mother was taken ill. Boilers burst, various structural repairs were found to be necessary . . . and so it went on until it seemed there was very little left that could happen. This was a wonderful time for trusting God as it were in the dark. Many asked the question: " Why is God permitting all this? How can the vision of what we all believe to be His plan for Chapel House be fulfilled?" Still, all through this time God was teaching me lessons that could not have been learnt in any other way, and I thank Him for every moment of it. Is it surprising that at the end of this testing time Our Beloved Lord again made manifest His boundless power to give? I quote here Bishop Loyd's words, spoken to us at a little gathering of friends of Chapel House.

" I was one of the first to inspect this house before it was taken over by Dorothy and it was at the foot of the stairs, after we had prayed for God's leading that the message came: ' Yes, let

Dorothy come here and I will bless it. . . .' I have not the slightest doubt that the message was from the Lord Himself. I am certain that Dorothy has been sent to start this Home of Healing, because God has also chosen this place to be a habitation for Himself. Of course the Master had started Dorothy from scratch, just as He did with all of us. She was in herself nothing, but years ago the Lord had laid His hand upon her saying that, just because she was nothing, He would now use her. To-day they had been listening to the story, and it was indeed a thrilling story and one which made them bow low down in worship of their faithful Lord. How wonderful it all was! He who could do no mighty works in His native city, because of no faith, was doing them here just because His children had faith to allow Him to have His way. That ", he continued, " must always be the keynote of this house of healing, an offering of everything to the Lord, so that He might work His complete will through us. Oh!" cried the Bishop, " if people could only be brought to realize what a wonderful spiritual blessing awaits those who put themselves wholly into the hands of the beloved! Here is the home of healing as a witness to this solemn truth. Here is Dorothy giving this message to the world in her daily life. How much she needs our love and prayers to enable her to carry on." The Bishop then referred to the additions made to the Home, adding that he had been almost shocked when a letter reached him in India telling him that these additions MUST be made. " Then ", he said, " came the faith and courage to believe that, if we were faithful the Lord would bless the new wing and its work. And now, as we see it all accomplished, we feel like doing nothing so much as to sing the Magnificat. Fortunately, Our Blessed Lord is at this moment in our midst to receive the full praise we have to offer."

The Bishop raised his hand, saying: " There is nothing like thanksgiving for keeping up faith. We have to admit that, although the Lord had led Dorothy through many hard times, He had sustained her in them. Just as He would sustain us all if we always remember that the Christian life must be kept clean and pure, a worthy offering to our God. We can read all about this life and its hardships in the beginning of the second Epistle to the Corinthians. But life is worth it, gloriously worth it! And so I want to leave this message with you. Dorothy asks for our prayers, that she might be sanctified and filled with the spirit of faith, and love, and Holy discipline, and that there might be no obstruction to this channel of the blessed life of our Lord.

"As we thank God for Dorothy . . . let our prayers be strong. . . . God is not going to let down the financial situation, but we must do what we can to put it on a firm basis. We are confident that God wants this Home to be a place of retreat and blessing for some of His sick people. And it would be sad if Dorothy had to say ' No ' to some of them because her financial limit had been reached and she could take no more, except at full fees. The Lord who has done such wonders, has many more things to accomplish in this place. We all want the cleanness, fullness, freeness and the beauty of this Home to be an offering put into the hands of our Beloved Lord for our Father in Heaven."

My thoughts go back in retrospect to 25th October 1930 when Bishop Hough blessed and dedicated Chapel House, and our Lord showed him that St. Michael's (the house in which I now live) would be part of Chapel House; and when to me it was shown that not only one, but *all* the seven houses were to be part of the whole. During the past years the causes for thanksgiving had been far reaching, and the greater part of this foreknowing has been realized, for to the original Chapel House have been added St. Raphael's, St. Faith's, St. Gabriel's, St. Michael's. In the fullness of time I believe we shall see added the remaining three—St. Anne's, St. Mary's, St. Joseph's.

There will not be time or space to give an account of all that has happened in the development of the work, nor of the countless numbers of sick and suffering folk God has healed and blessed. Sister Friend has included one or two outstanding cases which I feel it will help some to know of. I am continually asked: " What is the secret of these healings?" " What is the policy of Chapel House?", etc. The only secret I know of is that all those who come to serve God here . . . have one common desire—that His will may be done in and by them. The policy is that religion and medicine work hand in hand. I want to repeat here one of the addresses given by Bishop Loyd to a gathering of friends at Chapel House; for in his inimitable way he sets out so clearly, both the secret and policy of Chapel House. This address was subsequently published in Chapel House notes, a copy of which I have before me.

" I want to take as the central thought of what I am going to try to say ' The Big Life of Jesus '. That may seem to be rather a familiar, almost childish phrase. But what I wish to speak of is something very real and intimate, and is something which belongs to the great simplicities of the mystery of the Kingdom of God into which we must enter as children.

" What I mean is, that to be a Christian is to live a bigger life than our own, the Life of Jesus. Half the meaning and quite half the joy of being a Christian consists in living this larger life. And one of the great reasons why, in spite of the redemption which Christ has wrought for us, there is still so much gloom and helplessness in the world, is because people will not reach out and lay hold of the big, full rich life which is meant to be theirs in

Christ Jesus. We shut ourselves up in ourselves, and live just only our own trickle of life; and the result is, we either stagnate in a puddle of despondence or else lose ourselves in the sands of this life's desert.

" The point of being a Christian is that, through having Christ living in you, you are sharing, truly sharing, the lives of others, living in them, and letting them live in you. This applies very closely to the matter of Spiritual Healing and I shall probably best know what I mean by making the application.

" The only true healing power is Life. Drugs and medicines do not in themselves heal; they can only help. They may indeed be, and often are, absolutely essential if the life is to exercise its healing power; but always, and every time, it is the life of the body that heals and restores to health. Where there is no life in the body, medicines can be of no avail.

" Now in the matter of Spiritual Healing we are out to insist on two great truths. The first is that *all* the life we have is *one* life. That is to say, we have not one life of the body and another of the soul or spirit. The life which animates our bodies is the life we are living in our souls; it is not merely a material thing: it is spiritual also. So in seeking to heal the body, we must treat body and soul together.

" The second thing that one maintains is that the life which we live is not just our own life. Think how important this is! It means that, when Doctors have, by their surgical skill or their medical prescriptions, prepared the way for the life in my body to do its healing work in the fullest and most unimpeded manner possible, then the life which pours through the channels so prepared, is not just my own individual life (as it would be if my life were merely something material), but is the Big Life of Jesus, who became Incarnate that He might share His life with us, and now lives in us in order that we may share His life together. So, you see, what we are aiming at in our Spiritual Healing, is to get together and to join in pouring this larger life of the whole body into the body of the sufferers. We do this, of course, by prayer; for prayer is indeed the sharing of life. When we pray to God, we are sharing His life; and when we pray for others, we share His life with them. Then we use Sacramental means, either Holy unction, or the Laying on of Hands, to communicate to the patient our prayers and the life they constitute.

" Is it not a glorious thought, that we are able in this way to share the Big Life of Jesus with one another, in such simple and practical ways? And does it not make us feel indeed that the Kingdom of God is come upon us? And do you see how it all depends upon this chief thought, that our physical life is not just a material thing, but something spiritual in origin which we can combine and share?

" Undoubtedly we are here up against the mystery of suffering and pain which none of us can understand. But here again the thought of *sharing* may help us. Our Blessed Lord did not come to take away all pain from the earth, but He did come to share it, *all* of it, whenever He can get to it.

" I suppose that more than half the sting of pain and sickness lies in the loneliness of it, the single human body with its incommunicable pains or restrictions. But one of the purposes of Spiritual Healing is to ensure that that pain shall no longer be a lonely burden. Shared it cannot be while it remains on the physical plane.

" But in Spiritual Healing we take it up into the spiritual plane where it can truly be shared. It is thrown into the pool of common life. Again and again that life triumphs over it, and does away with it altogether.

" But it does not always do so. What then? Well, at least it has been found ever so often that the sickness, though it remains, yet, because it is being spiritually shared, becomes something quite different, and full of meaning and value.

" What a wonderful power some sufferers seem to develop of sharing the lives of others and of truly living in them! Just because of their sickness their lives become bigger; they are less shut up in themselves, and more fully partakers of the Big Life of Jesus. After all, what is health? If we speak materialistically we shall use negative terms, and say that health is freedom from pain and weakness. But if we start from the spiritual end, we shall say that it is that state of body which makes it the perfect instrument of the spirit. We grant that normally that should mean absence of bodily ills, and that we should always be seeking for health and soundness of body, if God will give it us. But if He denies it, shall we be dismayed? No; for we are more than mere animals, and even a maimed or ailing body can be the perfect instrument of the Big Life of Jesus which He is living to make us all one in Himself."

My convalescence was swift and complete, and in a much shorter time than had been anticipated I was able to cope with all that had to be faced. The house was full again, and there were a host of problems to be unravelled, not the least of these—the financial one. At this time a small property in Sussex was left me by a friend, the sale of which relieved me from pressing need. It was then suggested by Lady Palmer that a bazaar at Claridges would be a good way of helping.

Many friends of Chapel House threw themselves into this project. Princess Magda Murat promised to come and open the bazaar. The day arrived, a large number of people were present. Lord Daryngton, who was kindly acting as chairman, said: " I feel it a great privilege to be allowed to help the work of Chapel House, and it will, I hope, be possible, through our efforts to-day, to give some tangible and material assistance towards the futherance of this work which is being carried on there. . . ."

This hope, however, was not fulfilled, and it was made clear that though bazaars were well enough in their way, it was not the way God had planned for Chapel House. The result of the bazaar, in spite of all the work and effort that had been given to it, was not what had been hoped. Later, in His own unfathomable way, God showed us that He had His own plan as to whom He would use to help.

A man came from Africa to stay at Chapel House. He received blessing from God and wanted to give a thankoffering and had planned to give £50. When he was about to write the cheque God made him know that he must give more. He put his cheque book back in his pocket, and waited for God to guide him as to what he should give. Finally he went in to Chapel to pray . . . and there God told him to give £1,000. He wrote and placed his cheque upon the altar. Later in the day, on my return from a visit to a sick woman at Brighton, I was met by this man, his face shining with a new radiance and joy. He greeted me with, " Go and see what is on the Altar." This was another proof of our Lord's care and desire to provide *all* that was needed.

Soon we were again faced with the need for still more room, and with the need came the fulfilling. One of the five houses marked by our Lord in those early days of Chapel House was for sale. It was bought, furnished and subsequently blessed by Bishop Boutflower.

This house which was named St. Gabriel's was used to accommodate those who did not need actual nursing. It filled a great and long-felt need.

We were not left long in any doubt as to the growing necessity for yet more room . . . but there seemed little hope of this being possible. Again we saw the fulfilling of yet another promise. I was having lunch with my mother, who had been for some time confined to her room, when I heard that inner voice telling me " look out of the window ". I went to the window, looked out and saw nothing. Suddenly I heard " Tap . . . tap . . . tap " and saw a man nailing up a FOR SALE board.

This was the house that Bishop Hough had seen as part of the building on the day when he blessed Chapel House and which had been sold some eighteen months previously. I turned to my mother saying, " St. Michael's is for sale, and now God wants it for Chapel House." My mother's alarm was very forcibly expressed and she asked me if I were quite mad to attempt anything more. . . . However, in the space of a week it had been made possible through the help of two friends, to buy this house for God to use for the work He had planned to be done there. In due course it was furnished and blessed. On the day of blessing I was conscious of the sound of children's feet and heard their laughter . . . this happened subsequently again and again.

It was decided that I should move into St. Michael's with my mother, and have there those who sought, not so much healing of body as a quiet place in which they could keep a " retreat ", waiting upon God.

How easy it is to consent to doing some hard thing when it is not immediate, and how acutely difficult it can be when the actual moment comes for the fulfilling of such an undertaking! When the day arrived for me to take up residence in St. Michael's, after putting this off many times, I felt my courage fail, and three times went back to the Chapel asking God to give me courage. I went from the Chapel where, in the past years, I had spent much time with the Beloved. Here it was that all the difficulties and trials had been faced. Here it was that one always found strength, and learnt over and over again that " My Grace is sufficient ". It was here, too, that Our Blessed Lord came to me one night when kneeling before the Altar, waiting for His guidance in taking of a momentous decision. I became aware of His Presence when He laid in my arms a baby, saying, " Nurse this child for Me." As I knelt, the weight of the child became so heavy that I could scarcely sustain her . . . but in my heart there had come complete satisfaction. The vision passed and I expected to find the baby in my arms. It was then borne in upon me that this was something that God held for the future. I locked this in my heart and three years later realized its fulfilling.

There were other memories of wonderful happenings in this Chapel, which was the centre of all the life of Chapel House. Now the time had come when I should no longer be able to creep downstairs to spend some silent hours in communion with Him.

At length I left the Chapel and as I reached the door leading to St. Michael's I was conscious of Our Lord's presence, and heard Him say, "I will go with thee."

There was no longer any holding back, my feet went with the certainty that this was the will of Him whom I lived to obey.

The Holy Spirit filled St. Michael's; it was a happy, joyous place. All who came to it knew that God had set His seal upon it and had blessed it. When the Archbishop of Corinth came to visit us he said:

"As I came in and stood here, I felt Christ enter in to me." These proofs of the Beloved Lord's presence with us were given to strengthen us to meet the fiery trials which were before us.

There were rumours of the coming war, and none knew when we might be plunged into the horrors and anguish which would follow if war did come. When the blow finally fell, we were called upon to put into practice the Faith that, by the grace of God, had grown into knowledge. There were hard days and nights before us, but *always* we were kept free from fear. . . . Thanks be to God.

Soon after war had been declared, it seemed wise to plan, if need should arise, for some of the elderly patients to go to my little country house in Berkshire. So two garden rooms were hastily added, and a caravan purchased, thus making it possible to accommodate twelve people. The district was considered safe, and was certainly quiet at night. So it was decided to take those who wished to the "Ark" at Chinnor. A nurse and two maids went to prepare, and when the day arrived for the departure of those who had decided to go, we started off with a fleet of cars, an ambulance, and a van. It was a never-to-be-forgotten day, and indeed, was not without its humours and fun. We toiled all day and, amidst tears and laughter, by three o'clock in the morning they were all happily and comfortably settled in, and we returned to Chapel House.

The plan appeared to be working very satisfactorily, and the knowledge that those at the Ark were in comparative safety relieved our anxieties considerably. Like every one else we were up against difficulties and trials of every sort. . . . Not the least of these our constantly diminishing nursing and other staff.

Bombs fell all around us, and our nights were made lively by gunfire and falling shrapnel. I was told by the local A.R.P. authorities that a shelter must be built for the patients. So the lawn, which had been a great pride, was sacrificed, and a large and comprehensive shelter was built. It was very comfortable and complete with telephonic communication to the house. Some of the patients refused to leave their rooms, and decided to stay in their beds, no matter what happened. There were those, however, who chose to go to the shelter.

Shall we ever forget those processions down to the " Dorchester " as we called it? Ladies, whose ages ranged from forty to eighty, were clad in the latest style of syren suits and carried bags containing precious bits and pieces. One old lady insisted upon clothing herself in hat, veil, and gloves, saying, " Now I feel ready for anything!"

We had much fun, in spite of the horrors of some of those nights; and often the shelter rang with peals of laughter. Some of the incidents beggar description!

I must confess to dismay when I heard that my presence in the shelter was insisted upon. This, to me, was the last straw. Shall I ever forget the snores? In every key and tone they seemed to be, and after a few nights I armed myself with a long stick, which did valiant and able work in silencing some of these nightingales!

There were the nights when the shelter was flooded, and Marina and I baled at the sump between the volleys of gunfire and falling shrapnel.

One night an incendiary bomb fell, and set fire to the house which later was to be St. Anne's. We saw from the shelter my tall brother and Mr. Temple emerge to help put out the fire, which by this time was considerable. One was walking to the scene carrying a bucket of sand, the other a bucket of water. When they arrived at the road they saw a full-dress Fire Brigade, complete with fire engine, escape, etc. I will draw a veil over their remarks as they beat a hasty and ignominous retreat. . . .

Then there was the night when we saw Sister Friend escorting a dignitary of the Church, who was staying at Chapel House, visiting his wife, across the shrapnel-bespattered lawn to St. Gabriel's, with a large meat dish firmly perched upon his head. One had to see this to appreciate the humour of it. It would not be difficult to fill many pages with such incidents. But I must stop when I have told how Sister Friend, who had returned to St. Michael's to fetch something that had been forgotten, found the stalwart fire watcher and a retired Army Colonel, making themselves comfortable for the night under the kitchen table. Poor dears! they never heard the end of this!

The party at the Ark found life too dull, and decided to return to Chapel House, much against our advice that they should stay where they were in peace and safety.

We brought them all back, and shortly after this the Ark was let, and eventually sold. There was no longer any means of transport and the difficulties at Chapel House were as much as we could cope with. In spite of deafening gunfire and falling bombs, blazing fires, and every other horror by day and night, we were kept in safety, and seldom did fear rear its head amongst us, Thanks be to God.

We had many broken windows and considerable damage from blast . . . but not one of us received so much as a scratch.

We were often conscious of Angel protection. I remember, one night, having a great urge to go and sleep in my mother's bedroom . . . and found my bed next morning covered with splintered glass. This was the experience of many of us during the war.

We had only a skeleton staff, and even the skeleton threatened to vanish and leave us stranded without domestic help, with all the houses full of old and sick folk. However, we had no cause for dismay, for wonderful help came to our assistance, when four ladies, who had been patients at one time, volunteered to undertake the housework! What a revelation of adaptability, pluck and fortitude this was. They were a grand team, of not only dedicated, but joyous, willing workers. The houses shone brightly as a result of their labours, and through their timely help we were able to keep the Home open.

During the next two years were added the other three houses: St. Anne's, St. Mary's, St. Joseph's, thus fulfilling the original vision of Chapel House complete with its seven additions.

Perhaps the most wonderful of all the happenings of the past seven years was the coming of Anne, God's most precious gift to me. May I take you back to the night when I watched in prayer with the Beloved, when He laid in my arms a little baby, saying " Nurse this child for Me "?

Three years had passed since then, and now, during the horrors of sirens, falling bombs, wrecked houses, and children made orphans, God sent her to me, saying again " Nurse this child for Me."

She was sent to me in a wonderful way. My heart was open wide to receive this great blessing and trust. I pray God will make me worthy and give me wisdom and understanding. It seemed to me that there could be nothing left to desire, for Anne had completely filled any need there could have been in my heart.

She was christened in the Chapel by Father Barrett, who became her Godfather. Soon she became the delight and joy of every heart, and reigned amongst us as a little queen till she was seven months old, when the Beloved revealed to me that there would be eight more babies to be mothered and loved for Him. In a dream this was made known to me, and much to the dismay of many, I began to prepare for their coming. By the time the nurseries were made ready to receive them they were sent to me, and at the end of a year my family of nine was complete: five girls and four boys. I met great opposition from many directions and found unexpected resentment towards my children. However this was a small price to pay for so great a blessing.

They were both the joy and delight of my heart, bless them all! Legal adoption has made them my own children in every sense; may God make me worthy of this trust.

Mary, my loved and trusted maid, became Nannie, and together we cared for, and yes! toiled for, the darlings. They grew in stature and strength and were a perpetual and ever-increasing revelation of new fields of wonder and joy.

We had very little to contend with in the way of baby ailments. I remember no bad nights during their teething times. There had been a cessation of the bombing and for a long spell our nights were undisturbed. There were, however, some remarkable incidents of supernatural protection. One day, for example, I told Mary to bring the prams in from the garden quickly! She looked at me questioningly, saying, "There has not been a siren." "AT ONCE!" I replied . . . and as soon as we had got the last pram in a shell came whizzing down, the cap of which landed where Philip's pram had been! We have this relic still.

This was one of many similar experiences.

The days and nights of bombing returned with added vigour, and the questions of where to put the children during the air raids arose. I decided to turn the large dining-room into a shelter and house all the cots down there so that the children could be put to bed and, if need be, lifted out and put into the Morrison shelter in the centre of the room. This plan worked admirably. The children enjoyed these, to us, nights of horror and anguish. They were never afraid and asked often, " Will there be lovely bang-bangs to-night, Mummy?"

We learnt to sing many new nursery rhymes in our effort to drown the sound of the deafening gunfire without.

Thanks be to God, the children were brought through it all with no scar within or without.

At this time my mother was called to her rest. She had taken the children to her heart, and although she loved them all, her special delight was in Philip the baby, whom she adored.

Before she died, she had many visions of things to come, and many prophetic dreams. One day I remember her saying: " I have had a very vivid dream. I saw a big stone house, with a long terrace; there were children running about, and it was your home; many sick people were coming and going. It was a happy place and full of light. That is where you will go. I shall not be there, for I shall have gone on when this happens. . . . But God will bless and prosper this place." I replied: " But Chapel House is the home God has given me, darling." " Yes, I know, but it will all be changed later on." Nothing seemed more unlikely than the fulfilling of this dream.

It is noteworthy that this dream describes Burrswood, which later was to take the place of Chapel House as my home. My mother did not know of its existence; neither did I.

When the call actually did come for her, she was given one of the most lovely passings that I have ever witnessed. It was literally a falling asleep in Jesus. A short time before this she had a vision, during which her face was so indescribably lovely and shining with light . . . several people came into her room to pray. It was felt by all that the Beloved Lord was there. She regained consciousness after this, and I asked her if she knew me. She replied: " Yes, I am healed, I have seen Jesus. He told me things about you. He said, ' I will never leave her '." Those were her last words. How often in the days that followed I had cause to give thanks not only for those words, but for the knowledge that she was safe and at rest, out of all the horror and turmoil that we were called upon to face.

She had lived to hear in St. Michael's the sound of children's laughter, and the pattering of their feet.

Amongst the many letters of condolence and sympathy that came there were some from those who had heard that it was I, who had been called to rest. Sister Friend's sense of humour got the better of her when she invited me to read some of my obituary notices. I hope when the time comes my friends may be as kind to me as they were then!

The air raids were increasing in noise and fury, and I found myself wondering what the effect of all this might be upon the children later on. At the advice of several friends I sought to find some quiet place in the country where I could take them. I sought in vain, and after doing everything in my power, felt happy at leaving things as they were, knowing that if it were God's plan for the children to go to a place of safety and quiet something would happen to make this possible. This was exactly what did happen. The Lady Abbess of the Community of St. Mary at the Cross, who is a much-beloved friend of mine, wrote to me telling me of the possibility of a furnished cottage at Burnham, in Buckinghamshire. She asked me to go and see it, and then her, which I thankfully did. Mother had a great plan. She would take the owner of the Cottage, who was ill and lonely, to her Community to be looked after, and I should take my children to Abbey Cottage. This plan seemed to be a God-sent one, and we made all the necessary arrangements. How those dear Sisters (who were then at Nashdom, near by) toiled to make the Cottage ready for us. When we arrived everything was prepared, including tea. We all settled in and had a wonderfully happy time, in spite of the very restricted space. I had Nanny and another nurse to help me, and was kept in touch by telephone with Chapel House day by day, and night by night. Sister Friend and other members of the staff came down to visit us as often as possible, and I went to and fro between Abbey Cottage and Chapel House.

Those were hard days when every ounce of faith and strength were called upon, and though the flame of hope grew dim at times it never went out. We were all tired and worn *to the nth*, and our hearts were nigh failing from sheer weariness, when there came some signal blessing, bringing the certainty that all would be well.

During this time we kept on the altar in Chapel House a book containing all the names of members of the Fellowship, and those who were serving with the Forces, who had asked for our prayers. There were many wonderful answers to these prayers, which were so poor and inadequate in themselves but the lovely and encouraging fact was, what

Our Lord did with them. It reminded us of the five barley loaves and the two small fishes . . . what a silly offering to bring when there were five thousand to feed! but it was all they had to offer, and Jesus took what they had, and not only did He feed all, but had much left over. Shall we marvel then or doubt that He can, and does still work these miracles, to those who believe?

One night we were awakened from sleep by a queer and unknown sound. This came nearer and nearer and finally passed over the Cottage. Next day we learnt that it was a flying bomb, which had had the temerity to pass over our peaceful plot. These horrors continued to visit our surrounding locality. It seemed pointless staying away from home, so arrangements were made for us to return to Ealing, where we remained till the war ended. By the goodness of God we had been kept in safety, brought through perilous times. For what purpose? Surely none other than to be used by Him for the healing of those broken and scarred by the war. We had now seven Houses, three of which had been added during the last two years of war. For the last of these, St. Joseph's, we were waiting for permits to enable us to carry out the necessary work. Eventually, all this was done, and our beloved Bishop was coming to bless and dedicate the House on 25th October 1945. He was then the Bishop of St. Albans; near enough to visit us often. What an inspiration and unfailing help he was, as indeed he had been all through the life and especially in the early days of Chapel House. He never failed to encourage me to go forward in faith, knowing that God would not fail to complete that which He had begun; if only we were faithful. He was so practical and wise in all his advice, which was always given in humility; surely a mark of his sanctity and selflessness.

This year 1945 was to be an eventful one for us, and one in which many new friends were added to our number. Princess Marie Louise honoured us with her presence at our Reunion Garden Fête, and upon other subsequent happenings. The Princess took a very great interest in my little family, and always insisted upon visiting them in their nurseries. On one of these occasions Frances, one of the twins, asked her, "Are you really a Princess?" " Yes, Frances," replied Her Highness, " I really am. " " Then where is your crown?" asked the unconvinced little boy. " It is too heavy to wear often, but if I send you a photograph of myself wearing my crown, will you be satisfied?". . . A few days later the photograph arrived, and has lived in the Nursery ever since, and is one of our precious possessions.

On another of these memorable visits, the Princess asked Philip to show her the Children's Chapel. " What do you come here for, Philip?"

To face page 84

MISS KERIN AND HER NINE ADOPTED CHILDREN

asked the Princess. " To talk to Jesus and tell Him our Sorries, and get His bless," replied Philip.

We had a wonderfully happy gathering for the blessing of St. Joseph's, and amongst those present was Lady Ravensdale, who became then and there part of the plan and picture. I feel she will forgive me if I venture to quote from a letter she wrote me after this blessing. "As I compose myself to rest to-night, I hold in my mind's eye the picture of ' completion ' that to-day, through you, I had the privilege of witnessing; and that completion was your face, the children's, the Bishop's. How lovely this fulfilment flowers in the Spring of the first non-war year, with the horror of the world outside. Chapel House—you, St. Joseph's, must be the witness that there is still LOVE in the world, and battered humanity MUST find it in the radiance shed about us to-day. God indeed loves you."

This precious friend has done much in making possible the fuller flowering of God's plan for His little ones, to whom she opened and gave her great heart.

These precious children were growing up and the need of more help made itself felt. I was fortunate in getting Miss Harcourt-Williams to come as Governess. But the nine proved too much for her, and at the end of a short spell, other help had to be sought. The question in my heart was, " Who is sufficient for these things?" My children were all high-spirited, strong-willed personalities, loving and affectionate, without fear or shyness . . . a handful as well as a heartful. A succession of enterprising ladies came and left. They all loved the children but found the number too difficult and too overwhelming. The aftermath of war had added a problem, in that there were so few capable people free to come and help.

The Bishop felt that Ealing was not the best place in which to bring them up. But what was the alternative? It was quite evident that where they were, I must also be: and clearly my work was in Chapel House.

"God will find a way," insisted the Bishop, Elizabeth's Godfather, who had now become "Uncle Philip" to the children.

Life became increasingly difficult as the legitimate demands made by the children grew. Here at this point God's plan unfolded. Sister Friend came into my study one evening after visiting a patient in St. Anne's, and told me that she had met Miss Modin, who asked her casually whether she knew of anyone who wanted to buy a Country House to use as a Home of Healing. As Sister Friend was telling me this I felt drawn to make enquiries and rang the lady up on the telephone . . . making an appointment to go and see this house. It was the House I had seen in a dream some years previously . . . and I will leave Miss Modin to tell you how it came to be the country home God had planned for my children.

They were thrilling days that followed, and what a wonderful unfolding of the plan. I had previously approached the local authorities with a view to adding on a wing to St. Michael's, the plans of which had been presented: for one needed more room now that the children were growing up. We had waited for either the permission or refusal to allow this work to be carried out, and at this point it looked as though we might wait until the trump of doom before it came.

I had prayed for a sign as to whether I should continue to go forward with the possibility of buying the house in Kent, and on my return to St. Michael's after a visit to this house I found two letters which had come by that afternoon's post. One was the long-expected reply from the local council, refusing the permission to carry out the suggested enlarging of the house. The other letter was from a friend saying, " My very heart has warmed to the suggestion of the Country House, and I should so love to give some money towards the bricks. I so love children, and would in my advancing years love to help something where young things could grow up for Christ, watched over by you." Thus in this sure sign I knew it was God's will for me to buy this home, at Speldhurst, in Kent. It was called Etherton Hill.

The months that followed were full of every sort of difficulty, excitement, toil, joy and mirth, as we watched it all come into being. The move was planned for September, but at times it seemed quite impossible that the house could ever be ready. However, ready it was!

V

Etherton Hill

by Miss Gladys Modin

In 1930, the year that Chapel House was founded, Etherton Hill, seventy odd miles away, buried in the heart of Kent, was also bought for God. Neither the founder of Chapel House nor the purchaser of Etherton Hill knew of the other event; neither knew of the other's existence, neither dreamed of the eventual development; but in the purpose and foreknowledge of God, in the year when He called upon His servant, Dorothy Kerin, to found her work of Healing in Chapel House, Ealing, He also laid His hand upon the house He had chosen for the development of that work in the fullness of time, sixteen years later.

It was my father who bought the house, soon after my mother's death, in order that his children, his grandchildren, and eventually his great-grandchildren should be able to gather around him from time to time, and thus keep the family together.

And from the start how they loved the place! At once it seemed to become the family Nursing Home; everything seemed to happen there, from measles to the birth of the first great-grandchild!

It was manifestly blessed in the recoveries and the happy holidays, as also in the wider uses God claimed from it from the very first. Not a room that had not been prayed in, not a corner of the garden in which He had not walked and talked. And then suddenly my Father lay dying of bronchial pneumonia.

But he did not die, and when he recovered we talked much of the future of this already dedicated house, and planned that one day, in God's own time, if it was His will, perhaps it would become a real home of Healing, a house of rest for His sick and weary ones . . . and so the years passed by.

The war clouds gathered, the storm broke, and devotion to duty drove my father, then approaching his eightieth year to leave his home, and follow his firm to the West Country, there to devote his last years to " carrying on ", while the younger directors served their country. The story of how Etherton Hill was offered for the National needs, accepted, emptied of furniture, and finally rejected as " in a danger area "; and subsequently requisitioned by the Military and used throughout the war, is a story that does not belong here. Suffice it to say that we returned after six years' absence to find our once lovely home " crucified ", a shadow of its former glory, a wreck which we were advised to " pull down and forget ". What a home-coming for an old man already grievously scarred with the wounds of war. The Military were still in possession; we were in a cottage adjoining.

The day came when an official communication arrived notifying my father of the de-requisitioning of his home and possible re-requisitioning by the civil authorities, unless we made other arrangements for its use " within a month ". One month in which to find someone who wanted a house, caked in mud, dingy with dirt and black-out, bedaubed with the rough usages of war! What a hope! What a hopeless hope! . . . Busily we set about trying to redeem the bright promise of its beginnings, to find whether it were yet possible that God could have a place in His plan for this broken remnant of a home. How many sources we tapped, how many doors we sought to open but always with the same answer—too large, too small, too far out, too badly damaged. A fortnight of the month had passed, and we were beginning to feel that, after all, we were wrong and the home we had loved so dearly and God had blessed so signally, was no longer needed by Him.

And then it happened! So quietly, so naturally, so automatically, that it hardly seemed to happen at all!

Someone in sore trouble and distress needed the help and healing that only God can give, and anxiously we sought for the right place to send her, the right person to help her. For twenty-odd years I had believed with my whole soul in Divine Healing as revealed in the Holy Scriptures, but I had met no one and knew no one who had the gift of Healing. I did not know where to turn now for help for this stricken soul. I have always tried to follow a rule of accepting and acting upon a double witness. Therefore, after fruitless searchings, when two friends telephoned almost simultaneously to say, "What about Chapel House? Have you tried Dorothy Kerin's Home?" I knew my search was ended, and next day, my friend was safely tucked up in the one available bed in the Home!

How perfect is God's timing! I went to visit her there, and shortly after my arrival, the door opened, and in walked a stranger to us both, a lovely deep-pink hyacinth in her hand, and a lovely smile on her face. "Dorothy Kerin!" I thought. My heart pounded with excitement. I could hardly believe it possible that here in flesh and blood stood before me someone embodying all that for twenty years and more I had sought and believed to exist, if only I could find it.

"Is it Miss Kerin?" I asked, trying to appear calm and natural.

"Yes," she replied cheerfully, putting down the hyacinth on the dressing-table, and turning to the foot of the bed, as she said, " I love all growing things, don't you?" Bubbling over I put out my hand to say how thrilled I was to meet her, but she saw neither me nor my hand. She was looking at my friend and, reading her as she reads us all, she just gently said, " You need loving!"

I knew that I must leave them alone together, one of the hardest bits of renunciation in my life, for I supposed I should never meet her again! Twice more I went to visit my friend and on the second occasion I found myself introduced to Miss Friend, Miss Kerin's secretary. Eagerly I asked her to tell me more of the work of this wonderful place, and later, apropos of nothing in particular, I said laughingly, " You don't know anyone who wants to buy a Country House for a Home of Healing, do you?" And with that I left.

That evening, away back by my country fireside, the telephone rang and leaving my father I went and lifted the receiver. " Is that Miss Modin? Dorothy Kerin here. My secretary has just told me of your conversation about your house being for sale, and instantly it rang a bell. May I come down and see it?"

The hour had struck, the link in the chain had been forged. Within less than a fortnight of the " month to go " the furthering of God's plan was assured.

The soldiers moved out and the day arranged for Miss Kerin's visit had arrived. Never shall I forget that day! It rained till the grounds were awash. It blew so that an umbrella was unusable, and low, thick, rain-soaked clouds obscured every view. Few would have come, most would have arrived disgruntled and dishevelled. But when the appointed hour struck, a laughing trio were on the doorstep of our cottage, saying, " Never mind the weather, show us the house!" With sinking heart, knowing what " the house " would look like on such a day, in such a condition, I complied. "At least I have warned her," I told myself.

It was a humiliating moment opening the front door, and noting the reaction of them all. With a lump in my throat I led them around, and presently, unable to bear it any longer, I asked, " Is it worse than you anticipated?" She replied, *so* gently, " I didn't know it could be quite so bad, but I am going on with it . . . where can we talk?"

Before leading her back to my father, she asked to see the grounds, and pathetically we puddled and splashed over drenched hayfields which had once been lawns! Suddenly she turned and looked up at the house, and stopped dead in her tracks. " Look!" she cried. " It is the House I saw eleven years ago, even the white shutters are there!" And so the link was doubly forged.

During the months that followed, months of struggle against almost hopeless odds, she was to

To face page 94

CHAPEL HOUSE, SPELDHURST

be cheered on by " seeing " once again that same house now covered by Angelic protection.

To get the de-requisitioning, the licences through, the material and the labour for reconditioning, everything seemed impossible . . . yet it happened.

Nothing required seemed obtainable . . . yet it appeared. The date for the dedication was fixed, and there was no Chapel! No licence forthcoming, no way of getting one but no work of Miss Kerin's could be without a Chapel . . . that was unthinkable. Something must be done about it . . . a fortnight to go, and still no Chapel! Then . . . " a Red Cross Hut in the village being sold ". They had heard we wanted something for a Chapel, would it do? It was up in a couple of days, but was not weather-proof. " Line it with wall boarding? Impossible! Rationed. . . ." " Cover it with timber outside. Of course not!" Then someone found some un-rationed wall boards, someone else un-rationed planking.

Could it be done in time? Only if we engaged men for Sunday work. We would not do that? Sorry! then, no chance at all! Three days to go. The contractors on the phone: " Our lorry has broken its axle right out in the blue, and three men are free until it is repaired. Shall they come along and complete the Chapel?" And along they came.

Inside the house was a final rising tempo. One last supreme effort was being made to perfect the preparations for the dedication. Men everywhere, furniture everywhere, seeming chaos up to the very last day! And then it all vanished, and at ten o'clock that night we opened the front door and crept into the old house. A hushed silence met us on the threshold; we walked through the hall, and up the stairs and along the corridor. Virginal whiteness and beauty everywhere. "As a bride adorned for her husband," and outside on the tree-clad little mount, the log-hut Chapel, flower filled and beautiful, waiting for the consummation of the marriage.

The next day a great concourse of Miss Kerin's friends and well-wishers gathered to follow Bishop Loyd as he went from Chapel to House, from room to room, dedicating it all in triumphant joy to the Glory of God for the service of Mankind.

Small wonder that some saw Our Lord that day!

Not long after, my father passed to his eternal rest. But he had lived to see the fulfilment of all his dreams, to witness the resurrection of his beloved old home, to see it again filled with happy laughing children, now the beautiful home of a very gracious lady, God's servant, who, as its new owner, would be using it as he had prayed that it might be used, for God's glory in the healing of souls and bodies.

The day came when Miss Kerin called me into her study and said: " I have something to tell you, which may be a shock. And then she told me of the unfolding of God's plan, of the going on to Burrswood of the children and herself, of the closing down of Chapel House, Ealing, and of the re-opening of Etherton Hill as Chapel House, Speldhurst, as the Nursing Home. "And you ", she said, " will remain here for me. . . ." But that is another story.

VI

The Beginning of a New Chapter

Miss Joyce Weston, one of the ladies who had come to our rescue in the days when we were left almost without staff, and in whose capable hands so much had been achieved and made possible, went with me, taking Anne and Philip to stay for a week or ten days at the Cottage, to put the final touches here and there. These final touches seemed without beginning or ending, for we toiled early and late and seemed to achieve nothing but chaos and more chaos. But at last we saw some gleam of hope and the remote possibility of having the house reasonably ready for occupation. We returned to Ealing to collect the children and finally departed on this new adventure.

Out of this chaos came the " Virginal whiteness and beauty " to which Miss Modin refers. She has described it all so vividly, I will add but one thing, of which she was unaware. . . . Miss Weston had arranged all the flowers in her inimitable way: *her chef-d'œuvre* being a huge bowl of flowers most beautiful to behold. This bowl was about twenty-four inches across and held a vast quantity of water.

All was now ready and I awaited the arrival of my first visitors, when upon my ears fell a shattering, BANG! No one had noticed that the bowl had been broken and stuck together with some glue! . . . Water . . . and more water . . . everywhere; there was only one thing to be done, and our laughter, I fear, hindered our mopping up efforts; but by the time our visitors had arrived there was no evidence of the disaster.

The blessing of Etherton Hill, as it was then called, was one of the happiest parties I can remember; apart from the joy of it all, it was outstandingly picturesque. The beauty of the surroundings made a wonderful background for the colourful procession. The Bishop led, clothed in red Cope and Mitre; there followed Bishop Sawa and Bishop Nicholas Gibbs (of the Greek Orthodox Church); Dr. Langford-James, wearing his scarlet Doctor's robes; and a vast number of Clergy, robed; little girls dressed in white, and boys in blue Cassocks and Cottas, acting as Cross Bearers and Acolytes.

After blessing the little Chapel, which was hidden by trees on the top of a slope, the Bishop visited every room in the house and finally the gardens, praying that love, joy, and peace might reign in this place.

Lady Ravensdale cut the christening cake and after much rejoicing and thanksgiving our guests finally departed. It had been a wonderful day, and as we sat late that night going over the events of the day, we all came to the conclusion that our lot had fallen in a fair place.

It took a little time to re-adjust ourselves and to get settled in our new home, which the children loved. The cloud which loomed above us was the knowledge that as soon as things were straight Mummy would have to start going to Chapel House. I must confess to a sinking of heart myself for since God sent me the children five years ago, we had not been separated. And though I had the world's best staff and knew that the children would be cared for just as well in my absence as when I was there, it was a hard bit to be accepted: for the plan was that I should spend half my time at Chapel House, Ealing, and the other half at Etherton Hill. The experiment was not altogether satisfactory from either angle, and much time was wasted journeying to and fro. Life seemed to be getting out of gear, and was becoming more than I could cope with; the children were fretting and unwilling for me to leave them. The folk at Chapel House were all disgruntled and one day Sister Newall said, "It is like Hamlet without the Prince." I felt torn at times with the longing to be in both places at once. There was so much at both ends that could not be attempted for lack of time; my energy was getting depleted.

The chief desire in my heart was to do what God willed, but it was not easy to see what He might be asking of me. One day my problem was at once increased and, at the same time made clear, when Francis, with a sad little face, asked, " Why do you go and leave us, Mummy? They are not your children at Ealing, and we don't want you to go to them!" I tried to explain that the sick people at Ealing were there to be helped to get well, and that sometimes Jesus gave me a message for them . . . and so on.

Whereupon Francis clapped his hands, saying, " Hurrah, Mummy. I know how to change it all. I shall pray to Jesus about them and it will be all right." I asked Francis what he would pray, and the shattering reply was, " I shall ask Jesus to dead them all, then you won't have to go any more."

There was such feeling in the child's remark that I felt resentment might well find its place in that little heart.

After discussing it all with the Bishop, he said, " We will tell our Lord all about it; He knows what He is going to do, and He will show us if we really want to do His will." It was after one of these times of prayer that the Bishop said, " Little Sister, I feel that Our Beloved Lord may be going to ask you to give Him something that will cost you a great deal. But if He wants it, He will first give you all the strength and courage you will need. I know you will not fail Him. You will give Him all He asks, and in return He will give you Himself in the fullness of His Love."

" What do you think He is going to ask of me, Big Brother," I questioned.

" I think He may be going to ask you to give up Chapel House." It is impossible to describe my reactions to this blow, for indeed, blow it was; and at once all the reasons why this could not be God's plan hurled themselves one after another into my mind; this was indeed overwhelming. My heart, and mind, and will all rebelled. It seemed to me impossible that God could want this. He had inspired, guided, and made possible, the founding of Chapel House, where without doubt, He had healed and blessed so many sick and suffering ones. The houses were always full, and there was a long waiting list of those who wanted to come . . . surely this could not be meant to cease? The Bishop had made a mistake. After all, no one is infallible. This solution did not bring me any peace, for deep down, I knew that the Bishop did not make mistakes of this sort; he never gave advice unless he was sure. " Let us go and say the ' Our Father ' together." Taking my hand in his we went to Chapel. How long we spent there I know not, but at the end of the time, my heart was empty of all desire, save only that one desire—to do His will. Chapel House had been laid on the

Altar, and by the grace of God, I knew that whatever God should ask of me I should try to do.

The days that followed were anything but peaceful, and I was beset with every sort of argument against the giving up of Chapel House. I could get no clear guidance as to what was the right thing to do. At length the Bishop said, " Leave it to God; if He wants you to give it up, there will be some sure sign and you will know." So again I waited, secretly hoping that God would not want me to give up the Home, where He had worked so many mighty works of healing, and which was so infinitely dear to, not only myself, but many others.

This proved a fond hope, however, for a few days later I was asked if the Archdeacon of London could have the offer of buying Chapel House for a Diocesan House. This seemed to be an indication of God's will, and though this offer did not materialize, it was sufficient to make me start seeking to find suitable accommodation in Kent for the removal of the work. I looked at several possible properties, and exhausted the list I had from agents with the exception of two. These I planned to see on the same day. Burrswood was one of them.

I knew nothing about it except that it was big enough to afford the necessary accommodation. As soon as I arrived on the doorstep I felt sure this was the house and found it to answer exactly to the description of the house in my mother's dream, just before she died. I turned to the friend who was with me, saying, "There is no need to look any further: this is the house." It was dilapidated and almost as derelict as Chapel House had been, but I seemed to see it as it could be—something lovely for God to use.

The property had been chopped up and odd bits sold, including the two farms and cottages. But in my mind's eye I visualized it all complete again.

At this time I believed Chapel House, Ealing, would soon be sold, and that Burrswood would take its place. I therefore went ahead with the necessary formalities, and in a very short time had signed the agreement to purchase. Then the bomb fell and I found that the property in Ealing would not be required for a Diocesan House. This was indeed a problem, as I had gone too far with the offer to purchase Burrswood for it to be possible to withdraw. It seemed strange, that with only one desire—to do what I believed God was asking of me—that I should find myself in this plight. There must be some purpose in this, for surely nothing happens to those who trust God, that is not either willed or permitted by Him. In this knowledge I rested.

Soon there were several possible purchasers interested in Chapel House, who always for some reason or other withdrew. It was therefore decided to offer the houses for sale separately. St. Michael's

To face page 104

BURRSWOOD FROM THE AIR

was soon bought by a Doctor, who intended to use it as a Maternity Home. Then to my joy, a friend who loved Chapel House suggested that he should buy Chapel House and St. Gabriel's and continue there as a Home for elderly people. This seemed to me a God-sent offer, for there were those who had made Chapel House their home, and in their old age longed to be allowed to remain where they were. All this had been happily arranged, and thus our beloved Chapel House was to go on in the hands of a friend who would by God's help continue to carry on the tradition.

The date of this change over had been settled, and all the necessary plans made . . . when to our utter amazement we heard that the Middlesex County Council were interested in the property and were prepared to make an offer. This offer however proved to be so much less than the property was worth, that I was advised to refuse it . . . whereupon I received a notice from the Council stating that they were applying for an order for compulsory requisition of the property. I sought legal advice and was told that they, the Council, had powers entitling them to do this, and I was advised either to accept this offer to purchase, or to go to Court and have a case. The latter I felt would be entirely wrong, and in any event I could not seek legal aid with the object of gaining more money from the sale of Chapel House. So I accepted the offer, on condition that we had a speedy settlement. My friend who had undertaken to buy Chapel House and another of the houses, had actually paid his deposit, but unfortunately had not signed the agreement. My legal advisers informed me that this omission had completely deprived him of any right to fight for possession. And so it was that other accommodation had to be found for those whose intention it was to stay on at Chapel House, and the residue were brought to Kent.

The months that followed were full of frustration of every sort. The red tape of officialdom entangled everyone and drove them almost to despair. Where love, peace and joy had dwelt, there was nothing but desolation and chaos. The need for housing by the Local Authorities was acute and no one in their sane senses could have questioned this need. But in spite of this the months passed. Still nothing was done. There had not been even the payment of a deposit for the purchase of the property, and my financial commitments were soaring and piling up. There seemed no point of focus for attack, and one had to wait while the work of years was entirely destroyed. The houses were broken into and robbed, damaged through neglect, and allowed to go to ruin.

This state of affairs continued for the greater part of two years, when, at the suggestion of friends, I decided to have a question asked in the House . . . I owe a deep debt of gratitude to both Lord

Dowding and Lady Cripps, for all the help they gave me in their wise advice and sympathy. The suggestion of this question being asked brought things to a head, and in a very short space of time a final settlement was made. The financial loss was very considerable, and in all this one has had to learn that it is a counsel of perfection to be first . . . " as wise as a serpent, before you can be as harmless as a dove. . . ."

This seems a strange chapter to be included in *Fulfilling* and I had contemplated omitting it, but feel it is right to include it, for it is through this dark and very difficult period that God has brought us in to a fuller knowledge of His Love and power to redeem, not only ourselves, but ALL with which we are concerned. Perhaps one of the chief lessons I personally have had to learn through this is that Faith, however strong and real it may be, can *never* be dispensed with; and that, though one *knows* God *will* provide, there must be this constant testing for the increase of Faith, like the daily dying to self, of which St. Paul speaks. It is a thing we have never done with, and shall have to go on striving for as long as we live. May God help us to grow in Faith, and Hope, and Love, and give us courage to continue to worship and serve Him in thanksgiving for all His goodness to us. Of His goodness to us, we are never left in doubt.

The little family at Etherton Hill thrived and flourished, they loved this country home, and delighted in the beauties nature provided. They seemed to have an innate love for God and they surprised one at times in their understanding and wise sayings. We had family prayers, in which all the household joined. Often the prayers of the children reduced us, not only to tears, but to laughter; they were so delightfully direct with God, and had such fearless approach to Him in all their big and little requests.

I remember on one occasion when prayers became almost sadistic. We had heard that the governess who was to come to us was delayed on account of an accident. She had fallen on her nose. The child who remembered prayed that Jesus would make Miss Munroe's nose better. " But not too soon " came the request from one of the others! And Peter, whose turn it was to ride, prayed " Please, Jesus, don't let it rain to-day, because it's my turn to ride; you can let it rain to-morrow: it's John's turn then."

The children all know God as their Father in Heaven, and accepted this truth quite literally, as the following story shows. We had a Nun lunching with us one day, and Priscilla sat beside her. I knew she was embarking upon one of her questionings, and wondered what was coming when I heard her ask:

" Why do you wear those clothes?"

" Because I am a Sister," replied my guest.

" What is a Sister?" continued the determined Priscilla.

" It means that I have given my life to God, and this is my uniform."

" Our Mother has given her life to God, but she does not wear one," went on the child. "Are you going to marry and have babies? . . ."

" No, dear," answered the Sister, " I hope one day to be the bride of Christ."

" Oh, then, you will be a Kerin, because He's a Kerin. He's our Father."

This child has been signally blessed by our Lord, in the wonderful healing of a fractured skull. She had gone for her riding lesson with three of the other children, when her pony shied, throwing her on to the road. Incredible as it may seem an ambulance passed at this moment and took the child home. I had gone into Tunbridge Wells with the twins, who were to take an exam., and on the way home had a feeling of apprehension. I told the chauffeur that if the children had not returned we would go and meet them. As the car turned in at the drive I saw an ambulance at the door, and was told that Priscilla had fallen from her pony and was unconscious. I went to the child and found her in a pool of vomit, just conscious. She knew me and asked me to take her to my bed. After doing all that I could for the treatment of shock, I telephoned for the Doctor, who came later in the afternoon. He took one look at her and said, " I'm afraid she has fractured her skull: she must go to hospital." I was unwilling for this for two reasons: that this child had never been away from home in her life, and that I had a feeling that she was to stay where she was. The Doctor insisted that he must have an X-ray to show the extent of the damage, to which request I naturally assented, suggesting that the X-ray be done at home. The Doctor rang up an X-ray Specialist in Tunbridge Wells, who said that he could take the X-ray photographs at home, but not until the following morning. I was asked if I would take this responsibility, which to me seemed a far less one than taking the child to hospital. So it was decided to wait till the following morning. Whilst we were deciding treatment, etc., the telephone rang to say that Dr. Addy would come out that night. And finally we had his report: there was a fracture, and the medical prognosis was that if there were no complications it would take some six or seven weeks to heal.

I was kneeling by the child's bed, she was semi-conscious, and had complained of " big head-ache ". She was restless and feverish, and as I knelt by her side praying that God would touch her, I felt His power upon me, and laid my hands on her head. I was conscious of the Saviour's Presence. Later Priscilla opened her eyes and said,

" Mummy, did Jesus tell you to do that? cause all fwee headaches have gone—all fwee of them."

She fell into a deep and perfect sleep, and in the morning there was no evidence of any injury except a very bruised eye. She appeared to be quite well, asking for food and wanting to get up. When the Doctor came he was amazed and said that he had always hoped to see a miracle. But stressed the need to keep Priscilla quiet. However, by the end of the week she was playing in the garden, and in ten days time from the accident was up with me on my horse. I remember the Doctor saying to Priscilla, " I don't expect you will want to ride Lady again." " Indeed I shall," said Priscilla, " I shall ride her to-morrow."

As the days passed, the peace and beauty of this God-given place increased and one was conscious of an indescribable sense of expectancy . . . of what I know not, save that the unexpected was always happening and there were fresh evidences of the the love of God ever with us.

For years I had kept the early hours for prayer and meditation, and one morning whilst at prayer the urge to get up and go to the window was irresistible. As I looked out upon the garden, clothed in early morning mist, my eye was caught by a radiance of golden light about and surrounding the little lily pond. As I gazed upon this I saw a torrent of crystal water pouring from the side of the pool, tumbling into a cascade of sparkling diamond drops . . . the beauty and exquisite loveliness of which I can find no words with which to describe. I looked up and saw a stream of people, old and young, some on crutches, some being supported and helped by others. They all drank of this water from a small bright goblet. Then to my joy I saw some of them abandon their crutches; others walked unaided; and I knew the Healing of our Lord was taking place, and His power being made manifest. The vision passed and I was left with this vivid picture imprinted upon my heart and mind. What did it all mean? Perhaps something in God's plan for the future. I dressed and went down to the little pool and found a gentle little fall of water emerging from the side of the pool. And as I stood there, praying for the enlightenment of the Holy Spirit, it was borne in upon me that God would use this Spring as a means of conveying His Healing power, as He had so often used my hands. I told this experience to the Bishop and one other. The Bishop believed that as the number of those seeking healing increased, God might use this water, and suggested that I might give it to some who came to Etherton Hill seeking healing; but " that I must guard it as the secret of a King ". And several times I gave it to the sick, and each time the sufferer was healed. I then took some of this water to Chapel House, Ealing, and found that it had a most beneficial effect upon all those to whom it was given.

Suddenly the water ceased to flow . . . but I believe one day it will return. It is noteworthy that the little Chapel, which was built out of a tiled shed, was found to cover the site of the source of the stream of which no one had any knowledge. This Chapel has been greatly blessed and many have found, and do still find, healing of both body and spirit. I would like to quote here what has been written by some who witness to God's healing power through this water:

". . . At Chapel House, Speldhurst, I had a further sign of God's wonderful love. I had been suffering from double vision for some time when Miss Kerin offered me to drink the healing water from the pool in the garden. This I drank in Chapel, and the same night, just as I was going to sleep, a glorious white light passed over my eyes and they were completely healed; and so my life now is full of light and joy where once was despair and sadness. I must end this testimony of God's great mercy and love with thanksgiving."

PEGGY SIMPSON

"In 1947 I was suffering from Parkinson's disease and colitis. A mutual friend took me to see Miss Kerin at Chapel House, Speldhurst. On several occasions I was taken in to the Chapel; the atmosphere was too wonderful and holy to express in words. Miss Kerin prayed for me on these occasions and I received great benefit, but

I was not cured until the Spring of 1947. I received a message from Miss Kerin asking me to go and see her again. I went and was told of the healing stream which ran through the grounds of Chapel House.

" We went into the Chapel together, and Miss Kerin again prayed for me, and gave me the water to drink out of a silver goblet. It had a warm, soothing effect, glowing warmer and warmer as it descended. My cure was almost instantaneous and I have had no cause to visit Miss Kerin for healing since. It was a miracle, which I can never be grateful enough for, and for which I am eternally thankful."

A. L. Wood

" Dearest Dorothy—No words of mine can ever thank you enough for all that has been done for me. First of all it was just wonderful to be with you and the children. I enjoyed every moment with them. . . . Then came the Chapel. I can never describe how I felt or what happened and I don't know why anybody should bother about me. But as I was kneeling with you something happened, and when I drank the blessed water it glowed inside and I felt as if I was on fire. I wonder if others have felt this? The utter bliss of just being there is more than I can ever deserve. I am now back to earth amidst plaster, cooking, and scrubbing, but nothing seems to worry me now. I just feel filled up and able to cope with anything. Thank you again a thousand times and God bless and keep you always. . . ."

BRENDA VANCOURT

Burrswood, at Groombridge, was almost ready for us to move into, and the final exodus from Chapel House, Ealing, had to be faced. The breaking down of the plans there at the last moment, through the action of the Middlesex County Council, had left stranded those who had contemplated remaining there. These aged and sick ones were prepared for at Speldhurst and arrangements were made for them to come, with the remaining nursing and domestic staff as soon as we had vacated and made ready Etherton Hill to receive them.

I applied for permission to register this house as a Nursing Home. This was granted, and Etherton Hill became Chapel House, Speldhurst.

We moved into Burrswood in September 1948, before the repairs were completed, and began to wonder if the workmen would ever leave us. For one thing turned up after another, such as odd bits of dry rot, and the condemning of the electric light system, and a few other odds and ends of like kind. However, at long last the workmen departed from us and we settled down.

Those early days at Burrswood were in many ways a repetition of those at Chapel House, Ealing. As the days passed the sense of peace grew, and we knew that our Beloved Master dwelt with us, and this shambles, which was once a lovely estate, had suddenly, it seemed, blossomed into order and beauty again. It was to be dedicated to St. Michael, and Bishop Loyd was coming to bless it on September 29th, the Festival of St. Michael and All Angels. Bishop Loyd could not come on September 29th, and we had to have the Dedication on 15th September 1948. But we treated the day as that of St. Michael. There were a vast number of people present, and after the Bishop had blessed the Chapel and house, he gave a short address, ending with the words:

" Chapel House at Ealing has been a place where for years God has done many wonderful things. His work will go on here, and for that purpose is the blessing of this house.

" There are few places on earth where there is faith for God to do His mighty works, but here are people who believe that He can do them."

The Bishop then gave his blessing and, after tea, our guests departed, and we entered upon a new chapter in life.

The move from Ealing to Speldhurst was accomplished, and Miss Modin was in charge of the work there. I will not try to describe her selfless giving, not only of herself, but all that she has, and is. Her efficiency and tireless devotion to the work, to which both she and I believe God has called

To face page 116

BURRSWOOD

her, is one of the greatest blessings He has bestowed upon us, for which I am eternally grateful.

Canon Mallinson, Rector of Speldhurst, has been most good to us; he is always ready and willing to come and minister to the sick, and every other Monday comes to the little Chapel to celebrate the Holy Communion. We owe him a great debt of gratitude for all that he has done, and is still doing, for Chapel House, and for those who come there, sick in body and soul. I am sure that everyone to whom he has ministered will join me in thanking God for His gift of so good a friend.

During the next three years we realized the vision of Burrswood fulfilled, not only as a centre of healing which, by the goodness of God it has become, but as a complete whole again, with all the farm buildings, etc., restored.

Father Gilbert, the Rector of St. Thomas's, Groombridge, is our honorary Chaplain, and to him we owe a great debt of gratitude for his ministrations and help. Every Thursday he celebrates the Holy Communion at Burrswood, and gives sick Communion to any visitors who are in the house and unable to go to the Chapel.

We have been most blessed in having our beloved Bishop Loyd living here with us for over a year. When he had sufficiently recovered from his illness, he ministered to many who visited Burrswood seeking peace and healing. The time came when he was strong enough to celebrate the Holy Communion once or twice a week, and we had the joy of taking part in his thanksgiving to God for his restoration to health. I want to give here the greater part of an address he gave in this Chapel at a gathering of the Fellowship on October 25th, the day we always keep as the Birthday of Chapel House. We had put some new windows into the Chapel, which the Bishop dedicated upon this occasion; at the end of the little ceremony he gave the following address:

ADDRESS GIVEN BY BISHOP LOYD ON 13TH JULY 1951

"ALL thy children shall be taught of the Lord; and great shall be the peace of thy children." This comes in the Gospel for Whitsunday, where we have our Lord's own words to His Disciples, "Peace I leave with you, My peace I give unto you not as the world giveth, give I unto you." It is of this peace which our Lord gives to us I wish to speak now; because during my residence here in Burrswood for over a year, I myself have had abundant experience of the bestowal of this peace, and have also heard many others testify to their sense of it. It is a peace which all may have; and we shall seek it more and more. "Seek peace and ensue it," says the Psalmist, "for the eyes of the Lord are over the righteous, and His ears are open unto their prayers.". . . We all may have it, for the Lord Jesus bequeathed it to all of us. We are His heirs; and it is His peace which He won for Himself as man, in order that He might share it with us and all men who would believe on Him. Yes, He came to earth and sought this peace and ensued it as man, amid many sorrows and sufferings; and He gained it and made it His own for ever, though He was the son of man, who often had not where to lay His head. He did not acquire this peace, or preserve it, by remaining aloof in Heaven. Such a peace He never could have bequeathed to us.

Just so, the peace which we all know in Burrswood, and in Chapel House, as the Lord's own gift to us, is not the tranquillity of remoteness from life and its burdens, from its trials and its failures. . . . We have our Dorothy whose life testifies to this. . . . No, this peace is a precious gift which we receive from the Lord Jesus in the midst of our pains and distresses: and often He loves to bestow it most marvellously just when the burden seems to have become too heavy for us to bear. For the Lord Himself gained this peace by bearing the heaviest burden ever borne by man, the sin, the shame, and the sorrow of all the human race. And He found peace therein. He gained thereby this peace which is for ever peculiarly His own, just because He received that burden at the Father's hand, and bore it willingly and *gladly* for the love of Him.

Remember always that mere resignation is not a Christian virtue. The Christian virtue is glad welcoming acceptance of all that God ordains or permits in His Wisdom and love. This is the secret of this peace, Christ's own peace which He has given and bequeathed to us, the cross welcomed as Christ's blessed yoke. " Come unto Me, all ye that labour and are heavy laden," He says, " and I will give you rest. . . . Take My yoke upon you and learn of Me; for I am meek and lowly of heart and ye shall find rest unto your souls."

But can we accept the cross gladly? Is not self too stubborn?

Yes, again and again self is too much for us, and we rebel, or play the coward. But then the Lord Jesus, who bequeathed this peace to us, died and rose again; and now He offers Himself to be a new self in us. This lesson many of us have begun to learn here in Burrswood; I pray that knowledge and experience of it be shared throughout our Fellowship, that our joy may be full!

Do you remember how on the first Easter Evening, the risen Lord came to His disciples as they sat behind closed doors, and He gave them this same message of peace? " Peace be unto you," He said, and then He showed them His hands and His side, in order that they might be sure that He was indeed their crucified and risen Jesus. And also, no doubt, as they all meditated upon that scene, the sight of those nail-pierced hands would have reminded them how their Lord and Master had won that Peace for Himself and for them through the cross. " Peace be unto you," He said again, and then what did He do? He breathed on them, and said unto them, " Receive ye the Holy Ghost."

You must understand that that breathing upon them was not just an isolated act, peculiar to that first Easter Evening. It was the solemn inauguration of the new creation of the human race, whereby if any man be in Christ Jesus, he *is* a new creature. It was, I expect, a solemn inauguration of the new creation; and therefore it is also a revelation of our Lord's abiding relation with us. He is continually breathing into us the Holy Spirit, who is the Lord and Giver of Life, who gives us the perpetual human life of the Lord Jesus, in order that the Lord Himself may be our new self, and we may be able to say with St. Paul, " I am crucified with Christ, nevertheless I live; yet not I, but Christ liveth in me." But if this is so, if all the time Jesus is re-creating us, and making new creatures of us, by the in-breathing of the Holy Spirit, ought we not to take much more pains to be quiet before Him, so that we can become more receptive of this His gift of Himself and His Peace? This is what the Lord Jesus has been saying to me this Whitsuntide, in order that I may pass it on to you on this our Fellowship Festival day. And it is only right that I should attempt to do so, because it was here at Burrswood that He said this to me, and it is the love and the sacrifice, and the prayers of Dorothy and the Fellowship which do so much to make Burrswood and Chapel House what they are.

VII

Tesitmonies

WITNESS BY BARONESS RAVENSDALE

In God's earthly garden bloom many flowers, riddled with disease through lack of spiritual water; their beauty is withered with a mental and physical blight.

This little book contains the story of my dear friend Dorothy Kerin who truly walks in that garden with her hand in God's. I entered that garden through a friend who took me to Chapel House, Ealing, in the middle of the war. There I saw unfolding the miracle of God's work in those houses of healing, and in the nine children whom Dorothy Kerin had adopted. Ever since I would like to feel I was part of God's plan and picture and to be allowed to remain in that garden, and do whatever I can in spreading the news of Dorothy's work. I have truly seen wonderful things happen at Burrswood near Groombridge since those early days where—with her mortal hands—she has revived countless drooping heads with the heavenly dew, and sent them forth as glorious spiritual blooms to witness that the Heavenly Sower blesses the head and hands of his faithful gardener in Christ.

If you will read this little book and inwardly digest it, you will see how the author works in her garden: there is spiritual refreshment there for all and sundry if only they will listen to God's voice and have faith as a grain of mustard seed that he will heal in His own fashion.

Very often, as I have watched her work, strangling weeds of materialism and self-pride come in to mar the work she is endeavouring to do. It is we, alas, who often put our terms to God—as to how He is to heal us—and to Miss Kerin; if it does not turn out as we thought, we then criticize her work on us. Only the Lord of all life knows for our good what form that miracle of healing should take—it may be quite contrary to what we think is best for us—but I would beg all those who are weary and heavy laden to enter this garden. God has refreshed me again and again when I have been there. I know He uses Dorothy to refresh you, in the name of the Father who plants, the Son who prunes, and the Holy Ghost, who waters us in this place where there is no drought.

RAVENSDALE

WITNESS BY PRINCESS MARINA CHAVCHAVADZE

MY first introduction to Miss Kerin was in 1936 as a patient in Chapel House, Ealing. The many remarkable proofs of God's love and power manifested through her prayers made me ask to be admitted as a member of her staff during the War and it has been my privilege to work in her Nursing Home ever since.

Like so many others I had travelled along the great wide roads which by-pass the Heavenly City and had felt utterly perplexed by the numbers of religions which claimed to be the Truth. To my question, How can one tell which is the Truth, Miss Kerin's answer remains to me the touchstone of Christian discrimination: " What think ye of Christ?" The width of vision and freedom from prejudice against forms of worship other than her own, has attracted every kind of nationality and class around her. The gatherings of the Fellowship are a particularly striking example of this united diversity when members of every religion mix and pray together as friends. It is not just a bond that holds a group of people drawn by the same convictions, but the love that dispels antagonisms and overcomes conflicting interests of lands and temperaments. This surely is the great hope for the future when our swords shall be beaten into ploughshares.

I remember how the Archimandrite Michael Constantinedes, to-day Archbishop of New York, came to see Miss Kerin to find out for himself whether all he had heard about her was true. The answer came in an unexpected way. As I greeted him, he said to me:

" When I came in and stood here, I felt Christ enter into me."

These words and his expression will never be forgotten. That was indeed the answer: the Lord in Person had made Himself known.

When Jesus calls to us we are left with the free choice of saying either yes or no. Perhaps that is why He sometimes waits so long before making Himself known, in order to spare us the betrayal of refusing Him. When I reached Chapel House my collapse was due to despair for that very reason, and it took a determined Scottish friend to recognize my symptoms and pack me into a car and drive me to Chapel House. She did this very much against my will and when I enquired about my destination, she gave me this disconcerting reply:

" The Nursing Home is run by a remarkable woman."

That gave me a shock. The thought of a remarkable woman conjured up visions of a domineering Amazon with flashing eyes who would moralize and instruct me in everything; but I felt too weak to struggle.

Nothing happened in the expected way. On arrival I went to bed and waited. First came a tea-tray, then three hours later, supper. Towards dusk I heard a slight tap on the door and a small person slipped into the room and settled down on a stool at the foot of my bed. That I thought must be Dorothy Kerin. Some preliminary conversation must have been exchanged, but all I remember is the dam of silence which had been locked for years, suddenly bursting open to let a torrent of hidden fears and hopes pour into her patient ears. It was astonishing to me that this should happen with a stranger and one whom I was prepared to dislike. To-day I know the reason for this. Every visitor is received by her with prayer and our Lord paves the way for all her meetings. That night I slept long and peacefully and the following morning found the text for the day: " With the heart man believeth unto righteousness: and with the mouth Confession is made unto salvation." (Rom. x, 10).

Eagerly I read *The Living Touch* when it was offered to me by Sister Friend; and its message brought a blinding revelation. To learn from this book that Christ was real and present—not a detached Principle or a page in history, but a Person so concerned with our lives that He had shown Himself and spoken face to face with one who was ministering to me—that was the indescribable relief and joy.

The following day Dorothy took me into Chapel and there I received healing. I did not realize at the time that my condition of general collapse would normally have taken months to be put right; instead of which my health was restored in three days. At this point I feel bound to add that it is due to her influence that I later returned to my Church, the Greek Orthodox Faith, and re-discovered the beauties and mysteries of its teaching.

The week of convalescence that followed on the healing, was an unforgettable experience. The whole of life was transformed, the streets looked different, the trees and people round me all had new light about them. I was conscious of being cleansed and " without spot " but it also brought a terrible anguish at the thought of having to go back into the world and sin again. How could I ever escape temptation? Later this text came as a comforting answer after endless discouraging failures: "A just man falleth seven times and riseth up again." (Prov. 24, 16). Perhaps that is why it has been said, it is more a matter of courage than of time to make a Saint.

MARINA CHAVCHAVADZE

WITNESS BY MISS RUTH E. FARR

WHEN I came to Miss Kerin for the first time in November of 1942, I was, after a lifetime of almost intermittent illness, very near to despair—a despair so great that, had it continued, I think it must have killed me. Not only was I becoming ill again but my whole life had become so acutely unhappy and full of problems that there seemed no possible solution to it all.

At that first unforgettable interview in St. Michael's, Ealing, the despair began to lift. I realized that I was in the hands of an expert, the source of whose genius is the Holy Spirit. She listened to me patiently; she comforted and advised me; and then she warned me that there would probably be no swift healing for me. I gathered that it might be a long job.

About three weeks later I began that journey back to health as a patient in Chapel House. It was the most extraordinary journey I have ever made: all my pre-conceived notions of God's ways of healing people and dealing with them, were turned completely upside down. At times the journey was very painful; but Dorothy knew when the patient could stand no more, and she would help me over the bad places, bringing with her a sense of His Love and presence so delectable, that even after all these years I remember it with wonder. Presently I was sufficiently improved to begin to work for her a little; but I was still her patient and though I saw much less of her, I began to understand what it was to be surrounded with her prayers.

When this happens you seem to come very close to God. It is as if she takes you into His Presence, much closer than you could get by yourself, so that everywhere you sense that presence almost like a lovely fragrance enveloping and embracing you.

Gradually I grew stronger so that presently I was able to become a full-time worker on Dorothy's staff. At the same time something else was happening to me. I had come to Chapel House as a Quaker, but only a nominal one, for I had never been a good or enthusiastic Quaker. However, no one sought to alter this, but I found that as I attended the services at Chapel House there stole upon me slowly and unobtrusively the wish that I should be able to Communicate; and presently this wish became something so compelling that I could not rest until I had been baptized and confirmed.

From that time onwards I seemed to go from strength to strength. Eight or nine years have passed since then, and I look back with deep gratitude to God and to Dorothy, not only for freedom from illness and for the happiness which has come to me, but for the great privilege of being allowed to serve her in her work.

As a member of the staff you see things from a different aspect. You see things of which, as a patient, you were almost unaware. For although you see other wonderful healings, far more spectacular perhaps than your own, and you see the despair lifted out of other lives, you realize much more of the great burdens that Dorothy carries and the price of these things which she so gladly pays. Apart from her directly spiritual work, which is itself exacting and exhausting to an unsuspected degree, she is the mother of nine adopted children. In some ways her position is equivalent to a widow who must feed, clothe and educate those children entirely by her own efforts and earnings. Such is her serenity and the boldness of her faith in her way of living, that many, very many, of those who come to her for her prayers and advice and care, never realize for a moment the urgency of those needs. There is something in the situation which always brings to my mind the brilliant remark made by James McNeill Whistler during the course of his action against Ruskin. When questioned about the celebrated picture, "Nocturne," he confessed that it had not taken him more than two days to complete. The opposing Counsel then asked him in tones almost of indignation:

"It is in fact for the labour of two days then that you ask two hundred guineas?"

Whistler replied:

" No, I ask it for the knowledge of a lifetime."

That remark contains a profound truth which has its analogy in the spiritual life. For we come to such people as Dorothy with our illnesses and our agonizing problems and ask for her advice and prayers. These she gives gladly (unlike the artist she demands no fee for this) and it is all done so unostentatiously, so briefly, that one hardly realizes that in that half hour or so, one has reaped the rich benefits of a life-time's knowledge, and that moreover it has taken a lifetime of untold surrenders and mortifications to keep that little Channel in just those interior conditions which are necessary to evoke such wonderful answers from God.

RUTH FARR

WITNESS BY MISS MARGARET GREEN

THIS note is written to record thankfully an experience of Divine healing mediated through Dorothy Kerin. (" Spiritual healing " seems to have become an ambiguous term tending to get confused with Spiritualism, I therefore use the term Divine healing.)

In the autumn of 1949 I had a very severe breakdown and was in mental hospitals for nearly two years having repeated courses of electrical shock treatment. The doctors then said I was one of their failures and that if I did not get well within the next few months I ought to consider leucotomy. I had in the meantime become interested in Divine healing and was advised by a priest to ask Dorothy Kerin to have me at Burrswood which she immediately did. I arrived in July 1951 and by the following January was able to resume a few hours a week in London at my linguistic research work. I left Burrswood in March 1952 and have been living a normal life with increasing health ever since and am carrying on my work privately. (My professional appointment lapsed before I left hospital owing to the length of my illness.)

The important thing about Dorothy Kerin's work seems to me to be that, for her, and therefore those who come to her, our Lord is the Alpha and Omega of it.

Her faith stands on a rock from which by her devotion, she can rescue those who are struggling in a morass, whether it be physical, mental or spiritual. But it is the spiritual for her, which interpenetrates the whole and which is the basis for every kind of healing. Herein she goes far beyond both psychiatrists and doctors, useful as both may be on their own levels. And if anyone so spiritually groping and inadequate as I am can be healed by prayer, who could not be so healed?

I am not the only one whom Dorothy's prayers have saved from leucotomy. Another woman I know had been almost forced into it by one of our big mental hospitals. She managed to get to Burrswood and at once settled down happily and is now away and living a normal life.

MARGARET GREEN

WITNESS BY
MISS KATHLEEN BURKE-COLLIS

It was in 1946 that I first heard of Dorothy Kerin. I was then living a solitary existence in an old-world farmhouse in Switzerland. I was full of an intense longing to be able to serve my God. I would wander about in the forest of pine trees with which the farmhouse was surrounded, praying to God to give me the opportunity of being used in His service.

One day my friend, Miss Dorothy Arnold, who had just returned from England, assured me I must go to England as soon as I could, for a friend of hers, Miss Dorothy Kerin, needed some-one to help her look after nine adopted children. This Miss Dorothy Kerin, she said, was one of the most important channels of spirituality in the western world to-day. That was enough for me. Here was the opportunity I had been praying for. I packed a small suitcase and came to England.

It would be difficult for me to give my first impression of Dorothy Kerin, for I saw only light. I sat opposite her and I must have talked and she must have talked, but my only memory of that interview was of light. How I went out of the room and out of that house, I do not know!

At the end of June, 1946, I began my new work. In the six years I have been working for Miss Kerin I have seen many wonderful things. I have learnt what true service means and seen just how much can be endured for the love of our most Beloved Lord.

Reading the lives of the Saints one realizes that suffering and endurance are gifts, rather than hardships. If one did not realize this, one would find it hard to understand the incessant and continuous difficulties, worries, set-backs, problems, etc., that beset Miss Kerin's life. Yet through it all, even when we had but few drops of oil left in the lamp, when nerves were stretched to breaking point, her faith, her patience, her supreme trust in God is something that should set the world alight with new faith and hope.

Many are the miracles I have witnessed under this roof. Not only physical healings, which to my mind are the least important, but renewings of the spirit, the drawing closer of the soul to God, the conveying of a new value in life. I saw many lives around me that were meant to be happily employed in the service of their Maker and which had gone astray, bringing disease and unhappiness and tragedy in their train. These and cases of many other kinds I have seen guided and re-set on the path to God.

In a world that is fast becoming ego-centred, destructive and scientifically-minded, we are apt to forget that Jesus said we must be as little children to enter into the Kingdom of Heaven. Miss Dorothy Kerin is a living example of this pure and perfect Faith which is the only means by which we may enter the Kingdom. May she be given God's Grace and Wisdom, and the opportunities of expounding this great Faith and Love, to those who are seeking a higher path than their own material world around them.

KATHLEEN BURKE-COLLIS

MRS. ALMA FRANK'S WITNESS

IT was the eve of my flight back to America. A friend telephoned to ask me to tour the South of France with her. I explained that I had cancer and that I must hurry back to my physician. She asked me if I knew Dorothy Kerin? No? Well I must. I couldn't return to America until I did, she urged. " She is a person of great power; you only have to look at her eyes to know she is honest. . . ."

That afternoon found me at Speldhurst in an old, beautiful English house, waiting to meet Miss Kerin. Presently she came and after a few words of greeting, she invited me into the chapel. As we walked through the garden to the little Chapel I explained, " I am in no position to be healed, for since the age of twenty-two I have shed all forms of religion . . . besides, with thousands dying of this disease, why should I be healed?"

She nodded, and said simply, "I understand."

The birds outside the Chapel were singing a chorus such as I had never heard before, and the sun poured itself on and through the stained glass windows. As she opened the door a strong scent of fresh cedar wood embraced momentarily one's whole consciousness. It was an unforgettable moment.

We knelt; and after a few moments of silent prayer, the one I had come to see rose from her knees. Instinctively I looked up . . . what I saw kept me kneeling.

Her face was radiant. It was a radiance which I cannot describe. But if you think of the hills and valleys when dawn spreads the rising light of the sun, you will see with your inner eye what I saw with my physical eye. Dorothy, surrounded by radiance came towards me, I bowed my head and she laid her hands upon it. A current passed through them into my body . . . as long as it came her hands remained gently on my head, scarcely touching it. When it stopped her arms fell to her side, and silently she left the Chapel.

As I was leaving Miss Kerin asked if there was any time of day when I could lie down for a few moments in order that she could make a contact with me? I chose six o'clock in the morning. Standing with her hand on the door of her house she said, "I will always remember you." And then I was off back to London to continue packing.

It was nothing new to wake up before six the following morning. I had asked Miss Kerin whether, as well as lying quietly, I should direct my thoughts, and she answered, "You might say the Lord's Prayer." Accordingly, from a quarter to six I lay quietly in my bed repeating alternately the Lord's Prayer and a favourite poem. I was not looking for anything tangible by way of manifestation, especially as I had not asked to be healed, and had had previously no experience of spiritual healing. I aimed simply to quiet my mind. I did know through experience that a quiet mind, or, as I put it then, a controlled mind, generated energy. But there was to be more to it than that. Suddenly there came upon my head the same current that I had experienced the previous afternoon. I am not aware of its exact duration; possibly a minute or two. I looked at my clock: it was exactly six. The current must have started one or two minutes early; it was indeed an example of the unexpected, and it had a message of its own.

My plans changed. I telephoned Miss Kerin, intent upon asking whether I might stay with her for a week, providing my flight passage could be changed. But before I could get the words out of my mouth, she had exclaimed: "Wasn't that a wonderful contact we had this morning?"

My passage was postponed for ten days, most of which I spent at Speldhurst. This particular week of my stay happened to be an unusually busy one for Miss Kerin, as she was moving her household to a spot some few miles away. She had explained when I phoned that her time was to be so taken up that there would be for me only a few minutes morning and evening. The first morning she said to me, "You are welcome to the house and grounds, but I would advise you to remain in bed for the entire week." Nothing could have suited me better, as I was then finding movement of any sort difficult. By this I mean walking, rising from a chair, or even turning myself in bed. I realized, too, that I was beyond a spontaneous smile: that life had suddenly become clouded with grave effects, and that my heart was heavy. And by the time I saw Miss Kerin the following evening I realized one more thing: I could not stop making the effort to help myself. My brain and nervous system had responded to my will to keep going, and had obeyed so unflinchingly, that when I wanted them to rest, they *would* not. To Miss Kerin I mentioned this difficulty when she came in to ask about the day. The reply came in few words . . . "Be still, and know that I am God." "But how?" I asked, and added, "I am too used to making effort." Truly at that moment I felt myself in a very bad fix; "Be still" was exactly what I could not do. Moreover, at the close of this first day, which might have been a day of rest

I could say only this: "One thing I know: I *cannot* stop this making an effort." For a few seconds or so, as my memory has it, Miss Kerin seemed to be listening again to my complaint; then she lifted her voice (or was it my heart) and said, "Then make an effort not to make an effort." The first hurdle was jumped!

From that moment my brain and nerves took on quietness. The roses by my bed seemed to send their scent in great gusts into my nostrils, no matter how my head was turned. That night I awakened to the awareness of lightness lapping the heaviness of my body, the one seemed as of stone, but the lightness . . . as of breath.

Towards the end of the week I asked, simply, whether I were well enough to make the journey home, and Miss Kerin answered, "Yes." When a dear friend saw me in London to say "Good-bye," she exclaimed, "You are so changed . . . in one week!"

To my question as to what manner of change she meant, she answered, "Why, even your hands were the hands of a very ill person." Then I remembered their copper colour, their thin and hard look, and the large pale and blue veins. . . . Yes! healing had indeed begun; it was a process completed many months later. But that is another chapter, for I crossed the Atlantic again to be with Dorothy at Burrswood, St. Michael, and at Burrswood I discovered something else as well as healing.

" Burrswood is to me like the arm of God reaching down to carry out His promise," " Come unto Me and I will give you rest." Yes, I suppose Burrswood means to me more than anything else the carrying out of God's promises. I had read about them in the Bible, I had heard about them all through my childhood, and I believed in them in the same way as I believe the world is round, although I have seen little of its roundness.

In Burrswood the promises of love and healing become clothed in reality. I saw Love flowing, and flowering without fear, and I experienced healing. I cannot explain it all; it is beyond my understanding, even as I cannot explain the sun in the heavens, although it shines, and I see it shining. I can only repeat that love shines at Burrswood, whereas in many places it is merely talked about. Here it pours into everything and everybody around. When you leave Burrswood and you do not experience that same positive force flowing towards you and around you, then, by very contrast you realize this love through its absence.

Burrswood means to me this living manifestation of love and healing, and I have not known it or seen it anywhere else in this form or in this degree of reality. And when you also feel this healing power flowing through Dorothy's hands, this God-given channel, you begin to understand this love, hence to trust it more, to rely on it more, and to hope that perhaps you may be able to transmit something of it to others.

ALMA FRANK

WITNESS OF MR. THOMAS GOLBY

JESUS, replying to John the Baptist's question said: " Go and show John again these things which ye do hear and see. The blind receive their sight, and the lame walk, the lepers are cleansed and the deaf hear. . . ." And while we wait for His coming again how certain it is that His arm is not shortened. He is " the same yesterday, and to-day, and for ever ".

Surely it was not by chance that Miss Dorothy Kerin's books, *The Living Touch* and *Fulfilling* came into my hands but rather, I am convinced, by God's guidance in answer to prayer yet to be offered. For it was, indeed, at a much later date that I became ill. I was kept in bed nearly the whole of the winter of 1952–3 with intermittent turns and on 27th March 1953 I was taken to hospital by ambulance. While there, the fevers were overcome for the time being by medical treatment and their cause, a stone, was revealed by X-ray.

An operation seemed inevitable—not a light matter for one at the age of seventy years. The surgeon agreed, however, to my suggestion that it might be postponed for a time. So I left hospital on 6th May 1953 and became an out-patient for frequent X-ray examination.

No movement of the stone had occured when I wrote to Miss Dorothy Kerin explaining my condition and asking if I could see her. At her kind invitation I attended her weekly Healing Service on 12th November 1953 in the Chapel at her home in Groombridge.

Others who have been thus privileged have already spoken in better words than I can command of the deeply spiritual atmosphere which surrounds Miss Kerin in her lovely nursing home. No words of mine can adequately describe the impression one receives that our blessed Lord is close to her both when she is in Chapel and when she receives one for a personal talk after the service.

During the same month—November 1953—I received a letter from the surgeon at the hospital informing me that my recent X-ray showed that the stone " had moved a little ". Yet in spite of this movement I had suffered no pain. Then in January 1954, following a later X-ray, I received news that my film " showed no trace of the offending stone ". As those know who have had this trouble the slightest movement of a stone causes the most severe pain. I had suffered no pain whatsoever.

When Miss Kerin talked with me after Chapel on that memorable day in November 1953 I also told her how my wife had been in poor health for some time, Miss Kerin promised to remember her, too, in her prayers. Since then my wife has enjoyed better health than she had had for a very long time.

I wrote to Miss Dorothy Kerin as soon as I received the good news from the hospital and at the same time I explained my wife's improved health. In her reply Miss Kerin said, amongst other things, that she had " felt so *sure* that He had touched me that day in Chapel ".

She was *sure*. That perhaps is what was most evident in my talk with her after Chapel—the fact that she lives so close to our blessed Lord that as His channel for His blessings to flow to others she knows so surely His will for them. I, indeed, hoped but Miss Dorothy Kerin was sure.

The return of our blessed Lord in person is surely imminent. While we watch and pray for the fulfilment of this our hope let us thank Him daily for all His mercies in the knowledge that we may still ask in confidence for His healing, that His arm is not shortened, that His healing power still flows to us in generous measure through His appointed channels.

THOMAS GOLBY,
" Glenmore ",
Marley Lane,
Haslemere, Surrey

4th February 1954

WITNESS OF MISS JOYCE WESTON

My darling Dorothy,

In a few day's time it will be seven years since I was healed. I feel I should like to send you these few lines of remembrance to mark the day.

Chapel House opened loving arms to me when my mother's determination brought me there, sick in mind and body, and, after months of treatment, with little wish to recover.

Of your gentle patience in those early days I was well aware, but I did not know then, and now perhaps can only dimly understand, the extent of the sacrifice and might of prayer you offered for me. You taught me once again of the Love of God, and, in time, laid your hands upon me. I was not healed, and knew that my own lack of faith had prevented it.

Do you remember the joy with which I showed you I had been reading and had found in St. Matthew's Gospel, words, so startlingly simple, that there could no longer be any doubt?

" If two of you shall agree on earth as touching anything that they shall ask, it shall be done for them of my Father which is in Heaven."

The rest followed swiftly. It could not have been many weeks later that I saw you coming towards my bed one evening and asked you:

" Have you come to heal me?"

Instantly you laid your hands upon me in the name of our Lord and I was well.

I like especially to remember that you told me then that you would be in the chapel immediately below my room, upholding me with your prayers, and left me to realize the glorious certainty of the presence of Christ.

With my love and my gratitude always,

JOYCE WESTON

WITNESS OF EYE HEALING
MISS GLADYS MODIN

SOME eighteen months ago, after my eyes had been troubling me for some time—War strain, I called it—I decided that a visit to the oculist would be wise. I thought I just needed new glasses, though I rarely wore those I already had!

I came away from my appointment with the news that both eyes were affected by glaucoma, one very seriously so, and an immediate operation to safeguard the remaining sight was strongly urged. I have often wondered what it must feel like to leave a Specialist's room with a threatened doom pronounced upon one. Now I knew! From perfect sight all my life to threatened blindness—I, to whom blindness has been a lifelong horror! Yet, I was conscious of no fear, no panic. That in itself seemed a miracle to me. And when I told Miss Kerin she wasn't a bit worried either. " We will lay the matter on the altar, and seek a second opinion before taking any decision."

A week or two later, after having received the Laying on of Hands, I found myself, with Miss Kerin, in the presence of a very eminent London eye specialist. He put me through all the tests, confirmed the verdict, gave the same serious warning and advised an immediate operation—anyway on one eye. I told him of my faith in Divine Healing, and promised my decision in a few days, and after another warning that " WHAT WAS GONE, WAS GONE," and not to leave my decision too long, we left, and again I felt no shadow of fear.

It so happened that Miss Kerin's Healing Anniversary followed on this visit, her second birthday, a day kept with great joy and thanksgiving every year. I went over to Burrswood to the special Thanksgiving Mass, the late Bishop of St. Albans being the Celebrant, but I did not know till after that they had made me their " special intention ". But I had one disturbing thought. Was there anything I had not done that I should do to " fulfil all righteousness " regarding the laws of Divine Healing? There was something, and I asked Miss Kerin if I might be anointed, in fulfilment of St. James V, 14–16. The look she gave me told me I had done right, but she only said with joy in her voice, " You have made me so happy!" And very shortly after, I knelt before the Bishop once again to receive this wonderful Sacrament. Then Miss Kerin told me to " go ahead: to put myself in the oculist's hands, and leave it at that." I did as she had said, but asked that having had the full Ministry of the Church for Healing, I might have one final test before submitting to the operation. The appointment was made, and I went up, prepared now to accept as God's will for me whatever was decided.

When the tests were over, I said to the Specialist, " Well, here I am, what are you going to do to me now?"

" Not so fast," he replied. " Let us wait a bit, I DON'T FEEL JUSTIFIED IN OPERATING. You are holding your own. Come back in two month's time."

That was in April 1951. I still " go back " for a check-up every few months. I have not had the operation. The bad eye is no worse. The good eye has completely cleared up. The " impossible " has happened.

To God be all the Glory.

J. G. MODIN

WITNESS BY MRS. GEORGETTE VAN OOSTERZIE

AFTER a very serious illness which I had a year ago in Indonesia I was operated upon there and declared unfit for the tropics. We all went back to Holland, facing a very uncertain future. Since then I have felt more than ever, God's guidance in my life.

My husband, however, was offered a job in London and the man whose job he took over knew about our trouble, gave us Dorothy's name and address and told us about wonderful healings she had accomplished.

Burrswood was not far from our home and as my illness (which was malignant) had come back, I felt a great urge to go and see Dorothy. So on Christmas Day my husband and I went to Burrswood without having made an appointment, hoping to see and talk to Dorothy. As we entered the house we immediately felt the wonderful atmosphere that is in the house and that surrounds this remarkable person. We even found this expressed in the faces of the people we encountered there. Although Dorothy must have been very busy that day with all the children home from school we were immediately met and shown in by her.

She told us about some wonderful healings which God had done and that she was only " a little pipe ".

Although she did not assure me that I was going to be well again, she somehow gave me back my faith and courage and from then on I felt that I could face anything—even the worst.

She also asked me to mention a certain time in which we could contact each other through prayer and in which I had to be very still for a few minutes. I asked for half-past nine as that time is best in our very busy household and the children are in bed.

Dorothy is a most wonderful person and while she was talking to me it seemed as if she had the whole day to listen and help me.

After a while we went into Chapel which is an exquisite little room filled with the presence of God; and although the whole house was full of children and dogs not a sound was heard there. We knelt down and Dorothy prayed aloud asking God's help and assistance and after she put both her hands on my head, I felt a warmth going through the upper part of my body where the illness was and then I knew God wanted to help me and make me better.

I was so immensley impressed and so happy then that I had difficulty in restraining my tears. After that day I have been several times to see Dorothy and each time has been so glorious for me that I just wanted to go there again and again. At night, at the time when we had arranged for the few minutes' contact, I have often felt that same feeling going through me as I felt that day in chapel. I went on with my treatments at hospital in London but after some time the doctor told me that he couldn't find anything wrong with me any more and that I was completely healed.

I am so grateful that God made me ill and showed me the way to Dorothy and all that she represents! I pray to God to bless her for always.

GEORGETTE VAN OOSTERZIE

WITNESS BY LADY DOWDING

IN May, 1944, I developed chronic sciatica (and it's quite dreadful how much it hurts, and how exhausting it is to go on month after month with seldom more than three hours' sleep each night!).

Doctors and Specialists tried many treatments and drugs for eighteen months, but nothing made the slightest difference. Then quite suddenly help came. A friend told me of Dorothy Kerin, and arranged for me to visit her at Chapel House. As I sat awaiting her I imagined her large and aloof and quite frightening . . . and then what an amazing surprise to find her small, more full of love, wisdom and gaiety than any other!

I spent two such happy weeks at Chapel House, seeing Dorothy most days. And on my return home there followed one very bad attack of sciatica, and then suddenly it was gone and has never returned.

MURIEL DOWDING

6th February 1948

WITNESS OF MISS BEATRICE MIDGLEY

MY first visit to Chapel House in 1930 came in a very wonderful way. There, for the first time, I met Dorothy Kerin, whose kind help has meant so much to me ever since. A few days of indescribable happiness followed.

On my first morning our Lord granted me a healing, and made quite clear the blessed privilege He was bestowing in allowing me a share in this particular corner of His vineyard.

During many repeated visits, all greatly blessed, two miracles of healing which I then experienced are outstanding. On the first occasion I was confined to bed, suffering from severe nerve trouble. A few days later, on Whitsun Eve, came the Divine promise of healing through Dorothy. I asked for, and was granted, permission to slip into the Chapel for a short time the following morning. On the threshold He again gave me His message of St. John xiv, 27, and having ended my brief period of spiritual communion, He sent His servant Dorothy to me with His healing gift. The healing fire was indeed carried through her gentle hands and I knew I had been healed. My doctors regarded this speedy recovery as amazing.

The following year I was even more seriously ill. Again I was taken to Chapel House, and as I lay in bed one day looking at a plaque bearing the figure of Christ, that Dorothy had given me, Dorothy, in another building, and I, both received an assurance of my healing, which was granted the following day.

My greatest cause for thanksgiving for physical healing did not involve a visit to Chapel House. I had been taken to hospital for a major stomach operation . . . all symptoms and X-ray films indicating a deep-seated malignant growth. Dorothy wrote that she prayed our Lord would fill me with Himself and nothing else in the world would matter. Such was indeed the case, so that in the weeks that followed, all fear vanished, and in perfect peace, I left myself in His hands. After investigation I was sent home for a month, and a few days later Dorothy wrote that she had had the most blessed assurance that I would recover. At the end of the month a further X-ray revealed only the slightest trace of the disease and in another month there was no trace of it whatsoever.

Giving God the Glory for all His mercies and rendering thanks to Him for making Dorothy such a wonderful, loving channel of His grace, one learns that each recovery should be followed by seeking to learn His will . . . and in the doing of His will we find our peace and joy.

BEATRICE MIDGLEY

WITNESS OF MRS. G. A. POYNTZ

Two years ago I decided to ask Miss Kerin to help me and she recommended a Doctor. I went to Burrswood for examination, diagnosis and X-ray. This confirmed the fact that the trouble was a gastric ulcer of long standing. I was at Burrswood less than a week then and the pain, which was constant and at times acute, left me.

I arranged to return to Burrswood in three weeks for complete rest and treatment. I was X-rayed again and it was found that the ulcer had healed, though I was warned that I must continue the treatment of rest and quiet for some time to come.

At the end of nine months I was able to return to normal food and activities.

Two days after my arrival at Burrswood, Miss Kerin told me that I would not receive a miraculous healing, that it would take a long time, and that I must have patience, since I should be completely healed in time.

I am no longer young and I had dreaded a serious operation, so to me it was important to have regained my health without that. But even more important is the fact that while I was at Burrswood I gained that peace of mind and sense of nearness of our Lord, of which the world is in such crying need to-day and which it is so hard to maintain in the world.

I feel, too, that important as Miss Kerin's work of healing is, of equal importance is her message to the world of the imminence of Our Lord's second Advent, which she has given in her book *The Living Touch*.

G. A. POYNTZ,
Rose Cottage,
Hollingbourne

23rd July 1951

WITNESS OF MR. PETER RYLAND

DURING my stay at Burrswood I found that I had learnt more of Faith, of God, and of the teachings of our Lord than in my whole life. I found, too, that to-day and every day is the age of miracles. Moreover, I realized that the New Testament, so assiduously and narrowly read and studied in youth, is a living story and example.

Burrswood taught me that, and Miss Kerin gave me a daily faith, a standard to abide by, and observe.

Burrswood is a beautiful house, a house of laughter, happiness, and children, but above all, a house of God.

At His last Passover Our Lord said, " In My Father's house are many Mansions, if it were not so I would have told you; I go to prepare a place for you."

PETER RYLAND

WITNESS OF MISS EDITH CATLEY

MY mother had been suffering for a long time from an obscure form of acute neuritis which crippled her hand, and caused a deep and suppurating wound in the palm . . . no medical treatment helped.

She visited Miss Kerin and told her about it. Miss Kerin said, " When you go to Holy Communion, put your hand in the hand of Jesus and ask Him to heal it." My mother did so, and her hand immediately began to heal, and very soon the painful neuritis entirely disappeared.

EDITH CATLEY

WITNESS OF MRS. HILDA FARRANT

I WENT to a children's party at my daughter's home in September, 1947, and Miss Kerin and her nine children were there. She beckoned me to sit beside her whilst a conjuror entertained the children; so I took a chair next to her.

I had not been feeling very well, and for some days had been aware of an abcess forming at the back of my neck. I could feel the hard core of it, and could not move my head from side to side without feeling the drag of it. It passed through my mind to see Miss Kerin and ask for healing; but I decided not to bother her as it was a social occasion . . . so I said nothing about it.

When the entertainment was over I was astonished to find my neck was much easier, and I could move my head without pain. I told no one at the time, for I wanted to make sure that the hard lump would go, and after a day or two it certainly did, in the lovely effortless manner in which all God's healings are performed, without any physical remedies, or discomfort, or pain; it just faded away as if it had never been . . . and it never came again!

I knew then *who* had brought this healing power to me as she sat beside me that afternoon at the party, for she had put her hand on mine and whispered "*He* is here". Maybe she felt the love and admiration I have for her, and knew the harmony there is between us, deep down; though I am shy, and cannot express myself as others can.

HILDA FARRANT

WITNESS BY MISS EDITH CAUDWELL

WHEN my mother became very ill last October, my one longing was that she might come to Burrswood, because I felt that through Dorothy all things were possible with God. When she arrived on 14th November, having had a great deal of suffering, both mentally and physically, I knew that now she would be safe, and all would be well for her.

Of course, the first desire was that a physical miracle might happen, and my mother, who loved and trusted Dorothy, began to grow stronger. I do not know why God gave her this temporary blessing of regaining strength. When, quite soon, her strength began to go, she seemed to be given something to take its place, which we could only know as "the peace of God which passeth understanding."... The joy and gratitude with which she received her Communion each Thursday morning, after the service in our Chapel here, was wonderful to see.

One evening at the end of December, she told Dorothy that she had Heard His call, and she wanted to prepare herself for her journey. . . . During the five weeks that followed we felt that with Dorothy's help and prayers, she was just preparing herself and waiting for Him to fetch her.

It was the wonderful peace and serenity with which all those who came to visit her were impressed.

Although God did not give her the miracle we had hoped for, He had given her an inward peace and understanding which was a great privilege to witness.

When her last day came she rallied from a coma to receive the Blessed Sacrament, and to thank God in audible tones for all His blessings to her.

I am a member of Dorothy's staff and I should like to say that nothing that I could do, or give, could ever repay all that I received during those three months, and the infinite joy of knowing that my mother is now resting with Him.

EDITH CAUDWELL

WITNESS BY DR. HELENA KING

As a doctor who has had the great privilege of attending patients in Chapel House in the old Ealing days, I have known and worked with

Dorothy Kerin for many years. I have witnessed many instances of physical and mental return to health in young and old, and I most sincerely believe her work is in accordance with God's will.

HELENA B. KING, M.B., B.S. (LOND.)

* * *

On re-reading the foregoing pages, I realize how much has been omitted, the countless number of healings which have gone unrecorded, the many instances of miraculous intervention attributable only to the love of God, and passing man's understanding. Of all this I shall hope to write later if, and when, the plan unfolds. In the meantime, I humbly ask those who read this book to pray for the writer, that she may be hidden, or rather lost, in the Lord and Master, Whose Honour and Glory are her sole object in writing this book. May God accept, and use, this humble offering.

To face page 160

CHURCH OF CHRIST THE HEALER

APPENDIX

THE CHURCH OF CHRIST THE HEALER

Burrswood, Groombridge, Kent

" Speak, Lord, for Thy servant hearest "

The time is the 13th century; the place, a small ruined church on a little hill overlooking the Umbrian plane with the wooded slopes of Mount Subiaso rising behind. The sole protagonist in the divine drama about to be enacted: a young man, kneeling amidst the broken stones and weeds covering the floor of the church before a simple stone altar with a Byzantine Crucifix painted upon wood behind it. His eyes are fixed upon the image of the suffering Christ, and he is wholly absorbed in prayer. Suddenly, into the stillness and silence of this deserted spot a Voice falls:

" Build up my house for Me."

The Crucifix has spoken; it is a divine command, and Francis of Assisi, the prayer of whose entire life was that he might in all things do God's will, immediately set himself to the task of repairing the ruined church. This simple, unquestioning act of obedience was the prelude to a wide spread spiritual movement destined to renew the springs of Christendom's inner life, and at whose living waters we still drink to-day: the great mystical flowering of Spirit of the 13th century, an outstanding instance of the direct intervention of the Holy Spirit of God in human affairs at critical epochs in human history which can best be described as the Descent of the Dove into History.

We now come in the fullness of time to the 20th century. We are at a turning point in history, for it is an age of transition, the age of the atom, and mankind is taking a decisive step as regards its whole future. The mighty Wings of the Dove beat over the world as the Holy Spirit of God overshadows anew the destinies of mankind.

The place this time is a sanctuary of peace and beauty, a shrine of Divine Healing, standing in its own spacious grounds amid the fields and woodlands of England's fairest county of Kent, and known to thousands all over the world as Burrswood.

In the still hour of dawn, one morning in the spring of 1959, a woman, Dorothy Kerin, the foundress of Burrswood, is at prayer and in the course of that intimate communion between her soul and God, she is vouchsafed a Vision. She sees a church standing complete in every detail in what is the rose garden at Burrswood. From within this church, a wonderful golden light streams forth, lighting up everything it touches. As she watches, spellbound by the significance and beauty of this Vision, she hears the Voice she knows so well saying:

" Build this church for Me."

That same unquestioning obedience that we have seen at work in St. Francis has always been the outstanding characteristic of this equally dedicated servant of God whose divinely ordained ministry has over a long course of years transformed the lives of countless people all over the world. Like the Poverello, so dear to her, her instantaneous reaction to what she believes to be God's will has always been: " With joy will I do what Thou wishest ", and to this cry of the heart can be added for her " No matter at what cost to myself."

At the time of the Vision, there was no money with which to pay for building a church, but along with that unquestioning obedience to God's will as she knows it has always been this directing principle: that where God guides, God provides. Dorothy Kerin therefore went forward fearlessly with the project, ignoring the many counsels of caution showered upon her, with the result that the church was paid for as it was being built by the thanksgiving and love offerings of those who through her ministry have come to know the reality of the living Christ.

This beautiful House of God was dedicated free of all debt on May 14th by the Bishop of Coventry, assisted by the Bishop of Lewes, to Christ the Healer. Those who know Fiesoli, the little town on the hill above Florence, say the Church of Christ the Healer bears a marked resemblance to Fiesoli's ancient Cathedral. There is the same simplicity of line, the same air of quiet dignity and solidity, giving the impression that this church will withstand the ravages of time. Its bell tower and the cloister leading to it are Italianate in design and add charm to the loveliness of the whole.

Visitors are invariably enchanted with the exquisite beauty and taste that make of this Church a gem whose perfection in every detail renders it worthy to be offered to Him whose command brought it into existence. The furnishings belong to the period of the late Renaissance and are for the most part antiques acquired in Italy. The glass of the Rose window over the 17th century Altar is from Venice. The two panels on each side of the Altar are of St. John the Divine on the one side and on the other of St. Catherine of Siena. They are believed to have been painted in the workshop of Pietro Perugino, very possibly under the master's eye. Their authenticity is vouched for by the fact that for many weeks that section of the Italian Customs which safeguards the withdrawal from the country of its artistic treasures withheld permission for these paintings to be shipped to England. Half way down the nave on the righthand side facing the chancel, and standing on a bracket of the same period as herself, is a truly exquisite Madonna with Child at her side whose pure classic features and dignity of bearing belong to the school of Andrea del Sarto. Serving as lectern is a genuine baroque statue of an

Angel whose arresting countenance is of very great beauty. These are some only of the artistic treasures which adorn this " uniquely, mysteriously beautiful " Church of Christ the Healer.

As worshippers enter the Church from the porch, their first impression is of Light, light everywhere; and of Life, Life steeped in the peace and stillness of the Power of the Spirit. One instinctively feels this lovely church to be the Tabernacle of the Living Christ whose Presence is felt as a glorious Reality by those who come from all over the world to receive at its Altar rail through the hands of His chosen and sanctified vessel, Dorothy Kerin, the Living Touch of His Wholemaking. Services of Divine Healing, open to all who come in faith to seek a blessing from the Divine Physician, are conducted by the resident Chaplain every Thursday morning at 11.30 and on Saturday afternoon at 5 o'clock. It is at these Services that takes place the Laying-on-of-Hands by Dorothy Kerin. The Church depends entirely for its upkeep upon the thanksgiving and love offerings of those who worship there.

It is a significant fact that the Church of Christ the Healer is the first church ever to be built within the Church for the purpose of exercising the Ministry of Divine Healing, this sadly neglected legacy of the means to renewal of spirit, mind and body, bequeathed by the Founder to His Church when He gave to His disciples the divine injunction to " Go forth to preach the Gospel and heal the sick " in His Name and to His glory.

For nearly forty years, Dorothy Kerin has been a pioneer in this field of Divine Healing so vital to the future well being of mankind. She has been wonderfully used of God to bring about a new climate of thought in regard to the whole baffling problem of disease and suffering which to-day confronts the world in which we live. Her long life of spiritual ministry has been a fruitful demonstration that " God is the same yesterday, to-day and forever ", and that He has not gone back upon His eternal promise to abide with us to the end of time. Through the Power of the Living God, for whose Healing Life she is a divinely ordained channel, the sick are being healed of all manner of disease, faith given to the faithless, comfort to the sorrowing in increasing numbers coming from every part of our disease-ridden, fear-stricken world to be ministered to in her Home of Healing at Burrswood.

There is to-day a world-wide interest and growing faith in Divine Healing providing the only answer to the insoluble problem of the terrible increase in disease which is the baffling accompaniment to the great advances made by Science in every department of human endeavour. This new orientation of human thought and aspiration, we believe to be the direct result of the intervention of the Holy Spirit at this critical juncture in human affairs—a Descent in fact of the Dove into History—in order to open to humanity an avenue of escape from the maze in which we have lost the way to real health and joy and peace.

Every great spiritual movement can be traced to the use by God at its onset of some human instrument, chosen to give to the world that particular revelation of Himself contained in the special and divinely inspired Message which will best serve to quicken man's spiritual evolution at some given epoch. For the history of the spiritual evolution of mankind is the history of the operation of the Holy Spirit of God working in conditions of humanity under the divinely ordained laws that govern time and space. Dorothy Kerin's encounter with the Living God at the time of her miraculous healing marks her out to be such a chosen vessel to make known the truth that God's Healing Power is with us as much to-day as it was in those far off days in Palestine. It is her supreme gift that she brings Christ the Healer to souls, and in the light of that Healing Presence, darkness, disease and fear have no place. In churches and in Missions abroad, she is asked to give to congregations eager to receive it her God-given Message of Life, of Wholeness and of Hope. This inspired ministry is also exercised in the course of innumerable interviews and through the medium of a vast correspondence in which those who are sick in soul, as well as in body, receive from her the wise, inspired and loving guidance they stand in need of. The real story can never be fully told. This gentle, retiring, humble and lovely woman whose compassionate love for suffering humanity is a magnet that draws all who come into contact with her to awareness of the Living Christ's Power to heal, stands on the threshold of this New Age as God's signpost, pointing the way to that great promise of eternally renewed Life which is ours to receive in the exercise by the Church of her God-given ministry of Divine Healing.

From the Church of Christ the Healer a clarion call goes out to Christians of all denominations to heal the wounds inflicted upon the Mystical Body of Christ by their disunions, divisions and disharmonies, a call which will not cease to sound until there has come into being a nucleus of religious denominations foreshadowing the longed-for Union of all Christians whose allegiance to the Living Christ will be their paramount bond: that will have room for diversity of tradition, but sufficient reality of faith to participate in a spirit of common Christian fellowship in the commemoration of our Lord's Passion and Death.

In conclusion I quote these lovely lines from Frederic Myers' **St. Paul:**

> " Surely He cometh, and a thousand voices
> Call to the Saints and to the deaf are dumb
> Surely He cometh, and the earth rejoices,
> Glad in His coming who hath sworn, I come."

D. MUSGRAVE-ARNOLD